Solemates

Published by 404 Ink Limited
www.404Ink.com
@404Ink

Editing: Heather McDaid
Typesetting: Laura Jones-Rivera
Cover design: Luke Bird
Co-founders and publishers of 404 Ink:
Heather McDaid & Laura Jones-Rivera

Print ISBN: 978-1-916637-04-7
Ebook ISBN: 978-1-916637-05-4

Printed and bound in Great Britain by Clays Ltd, Elcograf S.p.A.

404 Ink acknowledges and is thankful for support from
Creative Scotland in the publication of this title.

LOTTERY FUNDED

Solemates

A History of Our Fetish for Feet

Adam Zmith

Inklings

Contents

Introduction
My Timeless Tradition

I loved feet before I loved fucking. It all started when I was really little. I was so young that feet were not a sexual desire for me at first. They were a special kind of curiosity. Feet were interesting to look at, and I loved to look. I watched out for the bare feet of cartoon characters like Fred Flintstone and I stared at the perfect specimens on the models in the Next clothing catalogue. One day, I wanted to touch. I was playing a game with another boy. I suggested that he play the king and I would be his slave. I told him it was my job to wash his feet. I held back from saying that I wanted to kiss them. I wanted to play with his feet, and I specifically wanted them to have power over me.

When I think about this story, I realise that I've had a foot fetish for as long as I can remember.

Exploring the history of our fetish for feet is another way to experience this curiosity. I'd like to understand why some of us have a foot fetish, and why we care about that. It's a desire that's well known and widely experienced. So I'd like to know all the different ways people enjoy feet, today and through history. I'd like to think about whether playing with feet is actually sex. I wonder why so many people find feet disgusting even though plenty of us want to touch them with our tongues. I wonder, in general, why shoes are important to people – from the collectors of valuable Nike trainers to the fashion obsessives who drool over the bizarre concoctions of Balenciaga and McQueen. I want to know how many kilograms of sweaty socks are sent between lovers through the mail each year. I'd love to hunt through all the kinky drawings from ancient Japan and the bloodied portrayals of Jesus's torment, and have feelings about the unique connection I have to foot-lovers from different places and times.

When it comes to kink, feet can be – sorry – a first step. As soon as I started to look at porn on the internet, I lingered over the photos of the guys who kept their bare feet in shot while they wanked or fucked. I found websites just for me, often called things like 'myfriendsfeet.com'. When I did start to get naked with men, I secretly looked at their feet. One of them was an amateur acrobat who moisturised his soles at the end of every day. He must have seen me watching him doing this one time. "I have to keep my feet tip-top," he smiled. The fact that he cared about his feet gave me permission to say how much I liked them.

It is openness like this that has led me to seek out experiences and take risks in pursuit of pleasure. I am promiscuous because I am curious. I've had adventures. I've learnt how I fancy bodies, their smells, their holes, their warmth and their electricity. I've sniffed armpits and pissed on people. I've fucked in public. I've dropped to my knees so I could beg for cum. I've kissed four people at the same time. I've had to stop when the oxytocin made me shake. I've been someone's good boy. I've hugged all night.

One desire has always persisted. I want to suck your toes. I'll just lay here on the floor, and you can place your sole against my face, and press. Hard. Your feet are powerful and, ultimately, I am not. I am the puddle that you splash through, and I love how you destroy me.

Am I a freak? Why does my brain fire up at the thought of licking a hot guy's foot? What the fuck is the point of that? And how long has this been going on?

The thing is, when you look, you see. I've noticed this in my own adventures. Sometimes feet are hiding in plain sight. We're barefoot at the beach and the pool. We paint our toenails to attract the eye. We choose footwear that says something about who we are, and judge others by their shoes. People wear sandals, and god bless them.

I've never followed the films of Quentin Tarantino, but I can't avoid them – not because they're popular but because they put feet into the frame. According to Tina Horn in her book *Why Are People Into That?*, "Tarantino may be pop culture's most well-known real-life fetishist."[1] Horn recounted her reaction to a scene in one of Tarantino's films in which a character rests her feet on the dashboard of a car, pressing her bare soles against the windscreen. "That's not just a shot staged by a man who loves feet," Horn told the friend who was watching the film with her. "That's the work of a fetishist."

Horn ought to know: she herself has a fetish for feet. As a sex worker, she's seen it all, including the wildest desires, but she opened her first chapter with feet because everyone knows someone who is into feet. If it's not you, you've probably joked with a friend when they said they'd welcome a foot massage in bed. More and more people are talking about feet, and their capacity for love. Celebrities are coming out! Ricky Martin, the singer and actor, told the audience of a TV talk show: "Don't judge me… I have a crazy foot fetish. Like, crazy. It's bad."[2] I watched him say this and I whispered to myself: *you're my brother.* And then I clicked on the next video suggested by YouTube, about a sexy actor who I fancied: "Darren Criss Got a Pedicure at Ricky Martin's House".[3] Darren explained how cool it felt to sit beside Ricky's Grammy awards and have his feet taken care of.

4

Apparently Ricky had thought that it would be nice to buy a pedicure for his house guests. How do I get into these parties?

Other celebrities are monetising. Kourtney Kardashian and her husband Travis Barker have regularly shared their foot love on Instagram. He praises her "angel feet", which are regularly the focus of their posts. In one, her soles are pressed against his smiling face.[4] In 2024, Lily Allen launched an OnlyFans account where she sells pics of her feet. "My toe daddies are very happy with the content that I am supplying," she said on the Miss Me? podcast.[5] Allen explained that after having been sexualised in the media from an early age, she was enjoying autonomy through her new business. "It's actually really fun to be in power and in control of something that I find so silly," she said. These celebrities are all very open, and that's a relief to me. It's an openness that has led me into countless conversations with friends and lovers and people 'in the life'.

The more I ask, the more I find out, and yet the more curious I become. I'm just a pretty small person at the front of a timeline, fudging my way through *la vida loca*. And so are people like Dug, a very soft-spoken man from Ohio who I interviewed for *Solemates*, who also loves feet, which he describes as "a basic human-nature interest".

Dug was four years old when this interest emerged in him. He remembers this decades later, when I spoke to him, as clear as the Midwestern sky where he grew up. One day, little Dug was playing with other kids and adults from the neighbourhood. "This one really hot neighbour caught me and kind of pretended to throw me to the ground," said Dug, remembering how he manipulated the man without knowing how or why. "I was such a precocious little runt. I said to him, '*Whatever you do, don't put your feet in my face*'." The man did it, playfully – and inside Dug a fire was lit for life.

At college, Dug went to gay bars and propositioned guys with the offer of a foot massage. "I was very uninhibited," he told me, and my heart trilled.

Another interviewee is Ajamu, who calls me "babes" and speaks with a gorgeous, friendly accent rooted in West Yorkshire. One day in 1992, Ajamu noticed that his lover had "a beautiful pair of feet". Ajamu took a series of photos of the feet, playing with the light, the textures, the shapes. He grinned, as he told me that he became hooked on feet forever.

Later, Ajamu was sleeping with a footballer whose feet were worn and bashed. "There was still something about that one that was quite beautiful," he remembered, describing how he sucked the footballer's toes. "He totally freaked out. Because basically, he never had his feet or his toes sucked before or worshipped. Lots of people still frown upon their feet being sucked."

The footballer allowed himself to feel some feelings, and he gave in to exploration. Ajamu played some more, and after a time the footballer enjoyed it. They both had pleasure together that way. Ajamu said, "For him it was a whole new experience…"

Not everyone is so easily open. Reed, a fun and fun-loving young woman with a gorgeous smile, tells me, "Feet have always been a thing for me." With a sense of sadness, this normally bubbly person reflected: "But it's definitely something that I repressed."

Repressing this fetish seems to be an experience that is almost as common as having it. It was easier to tell people I like dick than telling them I like feet.

I want to know where this shame comes from. I want to know why it boils over into things like the online reaction to the presence of feet in reality show *Love Island*: the scene of a contestant with a foot fetish licking the soles of another contestant was cast as a "violation" and "baaaaaaad vibes".[6] I wonder where this idea that fetishists are deceitful comes from. So I want to spend time in the history of our fetish, and with the widespread idea that feet are gross or inelegant when unadorned. Spaniards still talk about what happened at *Eurovision* 1983, where their entrant, Flamenco singer Remedios Amaya, performed barefoot and received nul points. Our collective revulsion to these cultural moments can probably tell us a lot about how we feel about feet – that many of us are so naturally disgusted by them that a fetish is impossible to empathise with.

But let's check that first; it's worth starting with the question that everyone asks me: *How common is a fetish for feet?*

Sexologists of the past have some answers. Richard von Krafft-Ebing, the first to catalogue our sexual desires, wrote in 1886 that foot fetishists make up a "very numerous class"[7]. Havelock Ellis wrote: "Of all the forms of erotic symbolism, the most frequent is that which idealises the foot and shoe"[8]. In the mid twentieth century, the great professor of sex from the USA, Alfred Kinsey, accepted that toe-botherers are "not rare in the population".[9] Kinsey also observed the special role that feet play in sex that doesn't even involve them, noting, "The toes of most individuals become curled or, contra-riwise, spread when there is erotic arousal. Many persons divide their toes, turning their large toes up or down while the remaining toes curl in the opposite direction."[10]

Later, in 1976, William A Rossi, published a book called *The Sex Life of the Foot and Shoe*.[11] In it, he built on Kinsey's observation with a theory about the enduringly common allure of the high heel: "It simulates the reflex position of the foot during coitus, especially at the point of orgasm or ejaculation. A tantalising question arises: Do both men and women subconsciously recognise or intuitively sense this 'sexualised' position of the foot in high-heeled shoes? And can this be one of the reasons for the sex-appeal of high heels?"

I am, evidently, not the first man to be excited about theories about our fetish for feet.

Social psychologist Justin Lehmiller, who asked 4,175 adults in the USA about their desires, discovered that men are more likely to fancy feet than women are. In fact, gay and bisexual men are four times more likely than straight women to have the fetish.[12] Publishing his findings in 2018, he also found that in general, one in seven of us have fantasised about feet.

Lehmiller's finding about queer men intrigued me, probably because I'm basic and it's always nice to be included. In researching this history I've tried to include people and places from a breadth of experience. But it's worth bearing in mind that I am a white cisgendered queer man living in London and who speaks only English natively. All these characteristics shape my work, but although Lehmiller found that queer men like me are more likely to enjoy feet, the fact is that this pleasure is enjoyed a lot, and in many different ways. Another queer man, named Mark, experiences his fetish quite differently to how I enjoy mine.

Mark buys used socks and boots from straight men; the pleasure comes from being allowed into the intimacy of another person's feet. Our feet spend entire days in socks and shoes, and these inanimate objects take on not just our foot odours but also their indentations and their secretions. These impressions are irresistible to Mark.

"That's my core interest," he told me when I spoke to him in his living room. The monochrome grey furnishings in his flat contrasted sharply with the cacophony of colour that escaped when he opened his drawers – scarlet, royal blue, magenta, patterns, different textures, bright white with dirt marks. "There's plenty of people willing to sell." His collection of used socks was ordered by type and colour, and it was clear that it is a huge, if secret, part of his life.

"We shake hands with each other all the time," he said. "You might touch a person's arm if you're a friend with them. [But] generally, feet and socks are off the table. There's a degree of intimacy and vulnerability for a person letting you in and to play with and touch their feet."

This is how our fetish for feet can be an honour as well as a pleasure. For Reed, as she leaned into her fetish, she discovered a new and specific way to enjoy it. "When I get tickled in the right way, it is literally like I can have orgasms," she said. Having her feet played with, especially tickled, is a "form of therapy". "I feel so sad for my past self. [I] repressed it for so long and never actually enjoyed myself. I now finally feel sexually satisfied."

People like Reed and others I have spoken to have seen their lives take fascinating turns thanks to their unusual pleasures. Mine has, too. Here I am, writing a book about our fetish for feet. Although I've collected friends with the same desire as me, and opened lots of Chrome tabs about our fetish, I've never properly delved into it. My curiosity is probably as deep in me as my sexual desire is – nagging, diverting, and blissful when satisfied. But there's something else pulling me into this work too, and I don't think I'm looking for scientific answers. MRI scanners are smart, but a time machine is cooler.

I love to travel to visit perverts from previous times. I found myself watching *Fellow Travellers*, a series in which two men start a sexual and romantic relationship amid the dark paranoia of Washington DC in the 1950s. In one scene, the one whose name is Hawk takes on a dominant role and makes the dorky one suck his toes. What a scene: the warm cinematography, the mid-century furniture, the beautiful men, and the *toes*. When the scene cut and I came up for air, I thought: would two men like that – in the 1950s, when homosexuals were being hounded out of public life, when WikiFeet hadn't yet gone live – really have sucked toes?

I care a lot less about the brain chemistry of these fictional characters than I do about the fact that this scene about the 1950s made it into a drama series in 2023. The palaces of ideas that we build around the silly things we like to do with our bodies are just as interesting as our desires themselves.

So that's why I have to go deep into the history of our fetish for feet. That's where this exploration must begin – as far back in time as possible. The journey is full of surprises. When I started looking into the history of our fetish for feet, I didn't expect to read about a plague in the thirteenth century. But let's travel there – into the wilderness (and wildness) of our shared history, our lives, our creations, and our desires.

Chapter 1
Walk Softly and Leave Prints

When you think about the history of sex, you probably think about diseased pricks and restricted cunts. Maybe the earliest dildo, made from stone 28,000 years ago? Or secret gays in the Cold War and whispering Victorian lesbians in bursting bodices? Maybe you can smell the body odour of the Baroque, well before the era of anti-perspirants? In looking backwards like this, you might not have looked down. Our feet were there this whole time. They've played a role in our sex lives in different cultures, across millennia. This chapter is a time-travelling tour through our historical interest in feet – and it's full of surprises.

Our journey poses some challenges. Ultimately, sex is just a moment in time when two or more bodies come together; even a recording of it is not the thing itself. Other historians focus on material objects – things like tools and mansions – and what they tell us about the people who made and used them. But sexual desire? Fetishes? I'm a historian in trouble, because these experiences are like love: indescribable and immaterial. This is their joy and their mystery. That's lovely, of course, but also really annoying when you're trying to write a history about it. Instead, all we have about fetishes in history are the traces that people have made about them: writing, pictures, films.

The second challenge emerges when you've got your hands on one of those representations: an ancient paint-ing, for instance, or a Bible story. In those, it's impossible to know what is sex, and how the people at the time thought about sex and feet. It's safe to say that a painting of a person putting a toe into the vagina of another person, when both are shown in ecstasy, is representing sex. Other examples are not so clear cut.

Some of the earliest footprints of this fetish rest in surprising places. Psychiatrist and researcher A. James Giannini began looking into the correlation of our fetish for feet and outbreaks of sexually transmitted infec-tions during the peak of the HIV pandemic.[13] Because that virus was spreading among men having sex with men, many of them got creative in how to share sexual moments while reducing their risk of transmission. If you speak to a gay or bi man who was sexually active during the 1980s and '90s, but wanting to avoid HIV, he may tell you that he attended parties where men sat around and wanked together. Or he may say that he got into kinky practices that had a lower risk of transmitting a virus than bum-fucking had. If someone is making you worship their feet, neither of you need to worry about passing, what was then, a deadly virus to each other.

Knowing that men were trying all sorts of inventive and low-risk sex practices to dodge HIV, Giannini wondered if others in history had done the same. So, he looked through a timeline of sexually transmitted infections over eight hundred years and found that outbreaks often correlated with evidence of foot action. Giannini noticed that when gonorrhoea flared up in the medieval period in Europe, poets wrote odes to feet.

There's an example of this in the book that became a mega bestseller through the fourteenth and fifteenth centuries, *The Romance of the Rose*. It was written in two spurts, first around 1230 and then around 1275, each part by a different author. This long river of a poem winds through the philosophy of love, and portrays a courtier attempting to woo a woman. It contains several love-drenched references to feet, such as:

"For I've heard so much good of you,
Such fine things, and of such virtue,
That I would give, and do promise
My body and soul, in your service.
And if I do grant all you ask for,

Naught shall I complain of more.
I will believe that tis my fate
To receive the mercy I await,
And, in that trust, I surrender."
With these words I bent lower
Wishing to kiss his foot…

In fact, feet had already shown up in earlier writing. In the third century, Greek philosophy teacher Philostratus wrote love letters. In one, "To a Barefoot Boy", he gushes about the beautiful shape of his beloved's feet. In another, to a woman, he implored, "Do not torture your feet, my love, and do not hide them … walk softly and leave prints of your own foot behind you, for those who would love to kiss them."

Once the Catholics got organised, it didn't take them long to get in on the kink either. The pages of Catholic monks such as Cerveri of Girona, the Monk of Montavidin and Guirat Riguier, are filled with toe-bothering – during the era that gonorrhoea swept through Europe. Giannini found that these poets also began to set down an idealised version of a woman's foot: narrow, with high arches and long toes. Giannini found that as the medieval gonorrhoea outbreak faded, so too did the fad for feet. In the sixteenth century, the threat was syphilis – and feet stepped back into the bedroom. Painters showed renewed interest in feet, and shoes began to show off toe cleavage, says Giannini, quoting from multiple sources. Sex workers advertised their nude feet to punters. The fetish continued until mercury began to temper down on syphilis. It's curious to find traces of your sexual desire popping up through history thanks to the parallel appearance of disease, but a trace is a trace.

Among these whispers of our fetish for feet in history are also stomping great clods of evidence. The scale of a particular cultural practice in China is probably unmatched. "For nearly one thousand years some five billion Chinese were immersed in a sex orgy with the female foot," proclaimed William A. Rossi in his book *The Sex Life of the Foot and Shoe*, in 1976. He dedicated a chapter to Chinese footbinding, drawing on the research of Chinese historians and physicians such as Chang Hui-sheng, and Howard S. Levy, who wrote an entire book on it in 1967, called *Chinese Footbinding: The History of a Curious Erotic Custom*. Levy's expansive study covers thousands of years of Chinese history and culture, features photos and drawings, includes interviews with women, and as it reveals the sexist and classist nature of footbinding, does not shy away from the sexual element either.[14]

In Rossi's own survey of our love for everything below the ankle, he described the long practice of Chinese footbinding as superlative, writing: "Perhaps nothing in history so convincingly demonstrates the reality of the foot's 'sexual nerves' and the role of the foot and shoe in the realm of human sexuality."

The practice of breaking the feet of young girls and binding them in cloth to change their shape and size originated, most likely, in the tenth century. It started among the elite, but spread to the lower social classes by the Qing dynasty (1644–1912). 'Lotus feet', as they were known, impaired women's mobility while also giving them the marker of status and feminine beauty. The practice continued well into the twentieth century. Although body modifications for status and beauty are common across cultures – from corsets to boob jobs, from large-gauge piercings to hair transplants, from intense dieting to, of course, high heels – what's unique about Chinese footbinding is the way it focused an entire set of social systems on the feet. It did this for centuries, and in a way that bound the women who did it to notions of desirability and sexual practice. Because the practice was so widespread and endured for so long, it is impossible to assign a single set of meanings to it. Binding was also variously implicated in issues of gender, class and sexism. For example, women's feet were often bound to prevent them from doing manual labour. They were kept in the home instead.

Over the long history of the practice it is also clear that for some people it was about sexual attractiveness – women with lotus feet were forced to walk differently, which changed their buttocks, legs and even the flesh around their vaginas, according to Taiwanese doctor Chang Hui-sheng.[15] Bound feet had a different scent to unbound feet. The book features stories of women penetrating each other with their lotus feet, and the long tale of a man known as Green Crane who travelled China seeking the pleasure that could only come to him via the "tiny foot": "When he had intercourse, he always grasped the lotuses tightly and bit them, not desisting until he had caused extreme pain."

There are countless interpretations of what lotus feet meant, but for Rossi, "This national intoxication with the human foot will certainly prevail as one of the strangest and most prolonged erotic love affairs in all history."

Europeans have had their own affairs, of course, via the high heel. From the sixteenth century onwards, wearing heels has also deformed peoples' feet, although less extremely than binding has.

Looking through paintings from all different periods and places turns up some other interesting love affairs with feet. In an epic artwork from Kota, Rajasthan the ruler Maharao Shatru Sal II is depicted as virile and powerful.[16] The mid-nineteenth-century piece shows a huge orgy, featuring men, women and animals, and includes the smug ruler himself giving pleasure to five separate women: one with his penis, two with each of his hands, and two final women are each enjoying a big royal toe in the pussy.

In Europe, gothic painters in the fourteenth century focused on eroticising the foot, just as their earlier peers had adored the breast. In a stark minimalist painting by Allegretto Nuzi from 1365, depicting Jesus's crucifixion, you can see John the Baptist lingering in his grief at the slain Messiah's feet. The great painter Caravaggio developed a style that transitioned art from the Renaissance to the Baroque periods; in doing this he took care to show Christ with dirty soles as a symbol of his earthliness. Through paintings such as the Entombment of Christ (1602–04) and the Crucifixion of Saint Peter (1601), Caravaggio made the point that these saints lived as paupers, helping others instead of elevating themselves. In one painting from around 1600, he depicted Saint Matthew with poor clothes and grubby feet in a commission for the Contarelli Chapel. But his portrait was rejected by the church and instead replaced by a more flattering image, with Matthew's feet clean and far less prominent.[17] The powers in the Catholic church had decided that dirty feet were unsaintly. However, one of the most enduring Bible stories backs up Caravaggio's interpretation of Christ's ethics.

In the olden days, in the Holy Land, before Jesus was in a Mel Gibson movie, and well before he was white, it was common for servants to wash their masters' feet. Jesus was a kind of master: people hung on his every word, especially the twelve men who were known as his disciples. In the story, Jesus and the lads went for dinner together one night. Just before eating, Jesus started washing their feet and giving them advice.

The image of Jesus washing the disciples' feet is prevalent throughout Christian art. The Italian painter Tintoretto made no fewer than six enormous and richly detailed paintings on the subject in the sixteenth century, depicting it as a scene of Jesus's humility and love. Christians came to love this story because Jesus did a servant's job. He was saying that there is no task too 'lowly' for a Christian to perform. He even used the towel he was wearing to wipe the feet clean: twelve disciples, twenty-four bare soles, 120 scrummy sand-encrusted toes imprinted into that towel. (And people think the shroud of Turin is valuable?!)

In other Biblical stories of foot washing, a woman is doing the work, and she's usually depicted as a 'woman of the city', or a whore. Very low, very dirty. When Jesus's disciples sat down for dinner, all dusty and dirty, and Jesus arrived with warm water and a towel – he was not only up-ending a class system, he was also inverting gender.

Other Bible stories use 'feet' as a metaphor for genitals. In Deuteronomy 28:57, when a baby is born it comes out between the mother's feet. Maybe that's easier to say than 'vagina'. In Ezekiel 16:25, Ezekiel condemns a woman who, ahem, "opens her feet" to everyone who passes by. And in the Book of Ruth, when Boaz had eaten and drank, and his heart was merry, he went to lie down at the end of the heap of corn. Ruth approached him, uncovered his feet, and lay down. The good book says: "And she lay at his feet until the morning". I'm told by a very reliable priest that this passage means that Ruth gave Boaz a blowjob. In the cornfield. Theresa May could never!

Bible stories are pretty famous, but there is yet another enduring tale that centres feet. In particular, it is about the powerful symbolism of finding the right girl via the right shoe. The fable of what happened to Cinderella has taken many forms across the centuries. Its roots lie in ancient Greece. In early versions, it's a sandal that pivots the narrative; in 1697, the French author Charles Perrault added the famous glass slipper. In whatever form it takes, the shoe represents the woman who is the object of desire for a king/prince/hunk. She is modest and beautiful, and her foot fits perfectly into a special shoe which somehow seems to sum up everything. The story implies that there is a power in footwear – or, in what it represents about a woman, and shoes are actually so often a symbol for the person. This is why people who like to be dominated by feet like their master/mistress to wear heavy boots or powerful high heels.

Another French author got involved in 1769: Restif de la Bretonne published a book called *Fanchette's Pretty Little Foot*, blending Cinderella with another story. The author was also known by the nickname Rétif and what's remarkable is that thanks to his story of a girl getting up to all sorts of japes with her pretty foot, the term 'retifism' came to stand for shoe fetishism. Writings like Rétif's are in fact full of adventurous feet and footwear. Some authors come across as philosophers of the foot – including Casanova. He may be known as one of history's great fuckboys, but Casanova also needs to be remembered as a man who appreciated a good pair just as much as a good read:

> The frontispiece of woman runs from top to bottom like that of a book, and her feet, which are most important to every man who shares my taste, offer the same interest as the edition of the work.[18]

In literature, feet abound. They are objects and play-things as well as symbols. Thomas Hardy showed a sustained interest in feet and shoes, especially in how they could reveal character. In 1872's *Under The Greenwood Tree*, the character Mr Spinks recognises the power of feet: "I know little, 'tis true," he says. "I say no more; but show me a man's foot, and I'll tell you that man's heart."

Elective Affinities (*Die Wahlverwandtschaften*) by Johann Wolfgang von Goethe from 1809 contains an episode involving the charm of the foot and the kissing of a beloved's shoe. In *The Brothers Karamazov* by Fyodor Dostoevsky, published serially in 1879-80, characters kiss feet, and one even writes a poem about another's feet in a kind of courtship. In a 1921 book from Iran about spells against demons, a reptilian feline in a little skirt licks the toes of a couple who are in bed and just trying to sleep.[19] A comic novel from Britain in 1995, *Footsucker*, by Geoff Nicholson, opens with a man describing how he tricks women into talking about their feet by pretending to be a market research analyst.

Just as authors have packed literature with feet in books from all over the world, shoemakers have flooded the market with their creations that help us to augment our fleshy inadequacies. Some designers have made a name and a fortune thanks to the way they've created new shapes for our feet: from high-end glamourpusses such as Christian Louboutin and Jimmy Choo, to the brains behind the running trainers that fetishists love to sniff, and the folks who continually reinvent the sandal in ways that drive toe-pervs wild. Most people who don't think about feet don't realise that whatever they're wearing down there will be of interest to one fetishist or another. Our tour of history shows just the ubiquity of sexy soles, whether flesh, leather, rubber or cork.

Half of Rossi's book is about footwear. The man was obsessed. He worked as a podiatrist and did jobs in the shoe industry and when he died he left behind a huge collection of books, papers, artefacts and memorabilia pertaining to feet and shoes. When archivists at Stonehill College catalogued everything, it took up 96 cubic metres of space in the archive. In his book from 1976, Rossi wrote that his fellow Americans were spending $11 billion per year on footwear. He would be giddy to know that by 2024 this market had grown to $91.5 billion, according to Statista.[20]

Rossi was not shy about making claims about the power of footwear. Although his interest clearly lay in women, he was open about how men and women alike drew on the power of footwear. "The more vigorous and aggressive the male libido, the more sexually aggressive the shoe styles worn. It's virtually an immutable law," he wrote in one chapter. And in another: "Men are still uncertain whether the greatest of all inventions was the wheel or the high heel. It's still debatable which of these innovations has had the greater influence on the course of human history."

These are the kinds of bold claims that men make about 'history'. Even if there is some truth in what Rossi is saying about the power of the high heel (which was worn by men in different periods and places), what his insight *really* shows is how present feet are in our history. All the different texts and paintings, stories and fables, reveal the endurance of our interest in feet, and how that is often driven by sexual desire. Wherever and whenever you look, we're playing with our feet. They mean something deep to us, as Italian shoe designer Salvatore Ferragamo knew. "I love feet," he wrote in his autobiography about designing shoes for stars like Judy Garland. "They talk to me. As I take them in my hands I feel their strengths, their weaknesses, their vitality or their failings."[21]

As Ferragamo implies, holding a person's feet, and spending time with them, is a very intimate act. In 1977, a book called *The Joy of Lesbian Sex* advised its readers all about this: "You can grasp her feet firmly; separate her toes with your fingers, and as though they were lollipops suck each toe thoroughly in turn. The effect is explosive: it's as if the nerves of the toes were directly connected with the clitoris."[22] This manual was a spin-off of the wildly successful book from 1972, *The Joy of Sex*, which hadn't included lesbian sex. It was written by Emily Sisley and Bertha Harris, and it featured an entire section entitled 'Big toe' which starts, perhaps defensively, "There is no portion of your body that is not capable of arousal or that cannot be used to arouse a lover." Sisley and Harris went on to hype up why lesbians might want to deploy the power of the big toe which, they wrote, "can be transformed into an active agent and be tireless at fucking in a way the fingers are not". The section also details plenty of other options that don't imply penetration.

Aside from a few mentions here and there, a tour through a history of our fetish for feet shows that most of the time feet are present in the bedroom they are not a fucking device. Usually they are massaged, tickled, licked, sucked, sniffed, and used to walk all over pathetic submissives in BDSM scenes. This is one of the most fascinating and enriching parts of a foot fetish, as you look through its history. Our interest in feet shows a remarkably versatile imagination, inspired by the potential of our bodies – all parts of our bodies – and how much we enjoy intimacy with other people. If history is a beach, we're all walking along. Glance backwards for a second and you can see a subtle but distinct track of footprints, vanishing into the distance.

Chapter 2
The Beard-Strokers

The nineteenth century produced lots of men who were bent towards science. They explored and collected, they categorised and analysed. They pulled apart from God, thanks to Charles Darwin, and many of them claimed an innate superiority in man. This fuelled male dominance and white supremacy, stealing land and building empires. Among these great Victorian men with their iron bridges and confected elite accents emerged the study of sex. As soon as they started to look into peoples' desires, they found feet.

The first of these men was Richard von Krafft-Ebing, a psychiatrist who published a book in 1886 with the title *Psychopathia Sexualis*, or *Sexual Psychopathy*.[23] Krafft-Ebing chose a scientific title, and wrote some parts of the book in Latin, because as he wrote in his introduction, his preferred audience was medical and legal professionals, and he wanted to discourage regular folks from reading it.

In the book, Krafft-Ebing wrote that non-white races are inferior and that homosexuality is a disease. I'm not going to smash into Krafft-Ebing for all the things he got wrong, although that's fair game – today, his work is no longer used by psychiatrists looking to help people – but in studying people and their sexualities, he reported in great detail what people were fantasising about and what they were doing in the late nineteenth century. These reports were never fully objective or comprehensive, of course, despite his attempts at scientific language – he failed to consult women or anyone from a class lower than the elite, for one. These reports are, however, incredibly useful to those looking to understand how our fetish for feet has been observed and shaped down the years.

On fetishism, Krafft-Ebing's book started broadly, noting the religious type of fetishism, where a person worships an object such as an amulet or a piece of bone that they believe possesses the spirit of their god. He described the erotic type of fetishism where a person gets sexual pleasure from the parts of another person, such as their hair, or even just objects they have used, such as a hairbrush. He then mentioned the story of Clisyphus in Ancient Greece, who violated the statue of a goddess in the Temple of Samos, "after having placed a piece of meat on a certain part", and a tale recounted in a French newspaper in 1877 about a gardener who was found shagging a statue of the Venus de Milo. Krafft-Ebing wondered whether to put these cases down to an unmet sexual need, or an attraction to an actual object. Then he delved into the case studies that he collected, including cases of fetishism for shoes and feet, which he classified as a "perversion".

Case 56, a "gentleman of high-standing", would hire a female sex worker once a month to flog the soles of his feet, calves and buttocks until he ejaculated. "The fact that he disdained coitus seems to point to the fact that he resorted to this method simply as a means to gratify his masochistic inclination and not as a ruse to restore potency," wrote Krafft-Ebing.

In Case 70, a man described the fantasy he'd imagine while wanking, that he was forced to wear girls' boots. He would smell the leather of a boot he bought for this purpose while wanking. His fetish for women's leather shoes started when he was ten and was still with him at age twenty-five. He also had the wish to become a servant, blackening shoes for "distinguished ladies", which would include putting on and taking off their shoes for them. This man had long harboured the desire to occupy a position of humiliation, and he speculated to Krafft-Ebing whether that was down to him reading slave stories during his childhood.

The book also reports the case of someone getting off by licking up the sweat between the toes of their partner, housed under the heading "Disgusting Acts for the Purpose of Self-Humiliation and Sexual Gratification". In hearing foot fetish cases such as these, Krafft-Ebing placed them adjacent to masochism, a desire and a practice to receive pleasure through pain or humiliation. Masochism ended up forming a huge part of his overall study – he even coined the term itself. To him, all of these desires were perverse. "Not infrequently fetishism occurs in the most various forms in combination with inverted sexuality, sadism, and masochism," he wrote. "Indeed, certain forms of body fetishism (hand and foot fetishism) probably have a more or less distinct connection with the latter two perversions."

Sentences like this are historically significant as Krafft-Ebing also coined the term 'sadism', the partner of 'masochism' in the dance of pleasure via pain and humiliation. Today, we often put the terms together in 'sado-masochism' or as part of the abbreviated acronym 'BDSM', an acronymic cluster that also includes bondage, discipline, dominance, and submission. Krafft-Ebing's descriptions of sadomasochism were among the many reasons why the Catholic church was outraged by his book.

The text also allied foot fetishes with these often darker and more extreme practices, as in the trampling and whipping cases. "It is highly probable, and shown by a correct classification of the observed cases," wrote Krafft-Ebing, "that the majority – and perhaps all – of the cases of shoe fetishism, rest upon a basis of more or less conscious masochistic desire for self-humiliation."

This hints at one of Krafft-Ebing's major innovations. Prior to *Psychopathia Sexualis*, psychiatrists, doctors and, of course, religious leaders saw sex in terms of morality. Some people were seen to do bad things because they hadn't been brought up right, or because they had an innate condition that messed them up. But, as Krafft-Ebing collected more and more cases of sexual diversity from people who talked in detail about their histories and their feelings, he proposed a different way to view desire. Where psychiatrists saw deviant sexualities such as foot fetishism as a symptom of a mental disorder, Krafft-Ebing argued how deviant sexuality was a general, continuous part of a person. He was right that our sexuality is a unique part of our bodies and minds, even if he was wrong to scream about perversion.

Krafft-Ebing's book is a paradox. It sold very well, and there's a theory that it led to an uptick in sales of Latin dictionaries. It went through twelve editions. It is remarkable in its candour and the extremity of some of the sexual desires and practices it features. It influenced discussions about sex and sexuality among the beard-stroking elite for decades, and it remains a significant historical text. But not everyone wanted to read tales of sexual diversity. The editors of the British Medical Journal held their noses and finally began to discuss *Psychopathia*

Sexualis in 1893, seven years after its first edition – only because it was so famous by that point that it would be weird to ignore it. They even questioned why the book contained any English at all, writing: "Better if it had been written entirely in Latin, and thus veiled in the decent obscurity of a dead language."[24]

Krafft-Ebing's book brought 'perverse' activities out into the open, to the attention of fellow scientists and men of learned institutions. The activities were also a part of the growth in erotic art and literature from the same time, such as *The Pearl*, a dirty magazine founded in 1879. One story from the edition dated August 1880 features a character named Lady Pokingham who reclines in front of a suitor, Charles. The lady narrates: "[I] opened my legs whilst his hands opened the slit in my drawers and exposed the lips of my cunt to view. His mouth was glued to it in a moment, and ah! oh! how his lascivious tongue made me spend in a second or two whilst my unslippered foot was rolling his prick on his thigh."

No doubt the editors of the *British Medical Journal* would have preferred that in Latin, too. But magazines like *The Pearl*, before it was shut down for obscenity in 1881,[25] were depicting real fantasies, and so Krafft-Ebing knew he had to talk about them. Other beard-strokers began to join in too, from adjacent fields of study. When *Psychopathia Sexualis* came out, a psychologist from the USA called G. Stanley Hall was setting up the first laboratory for psychology, the *American Journal of Psychology* and the American Psychological Association. He was its first president. As well as helping to establish his field in the USA, Hall also spent time doing research at Johns Hopkins University, America's first research University, in Baltimore.

In 1895, Hall collected and assembled data that sought to understand how a sense of self arose in young children. In total, Hall claimed, his project represented nearly a thousand people. It revealed that children are fascinated by feet. "Some children become greatly excited whenever their feet are exposed, and especially whenever the foot gear is removed," Hall wrote in his paper, published in 1898 in the *American Journal of Psychology*.[26] "Many are described as playing with them as if fascinated by strange, newly-discovered toys. They pick them up and try to throw them away, or out of the cradle, or bring them to the mouth, where all things tend to go. Then comes the stage of toe-sucking, which sometimes as early as three months becomes persistent and troublesome."

Hall's paper said that some children treat their feet as separate creatures, offering them food or otherwise seeking to gratify them as if they had an ego that was all their own. He added that some children howl with laughter when they are tickled on their feet, and some hate the idea of having to wear shoes or socks. Some children develop a special interest in the feet of others, "sometimes expressing surprise that the pinch of the mother's toe hurts her and not the child".

In his paper, Hall wondered whether children's common fascination with feet could be linked to, in some, a later fetishism. Rather disparagingly, he wrote: "One cannot read these plain and homely data without querying whether some of these exacerbations of this group of experiences may be laying some of the psycho-physical foundations for the foot fetishisms which may later appear in degenerates after the dawn of sexual maturity." There you have it: a happy baby with a foot in the mouth is troublesome and very probably a degenerate.

The overlap here between psychology and what was becoming a field of sexology is important. Krafft-Ebing's book had been an exercise in establishing sexology as a distinct practice allied to psychology and medicine. In England, researcher Havelock Ellis published *Sexual Inversion* in 1897, which describes sex between men in terms that did not characterise them as diseased or immoral.[27] "The stream of nature still flows into the bent channel of sexual inversion," he proclaimed boldly, hoping the doctors and the Catholics in the back could hear him, "and still runs according to law."

In the same year in Germany, a medical doctor named Magnus Hirschfeld founded what is now considered to be the world's first gay rights organisation, the Scientific Humanitarian Committee. Hirschfeld's group grew out of his work in supporting the wellbeing of homosexual men and trans people who were maligned by society, and his and others' campaigns to lift the legal ban on sodomy. Ellis continued to add volumes to his growing collection of work on the *Psychology of Sex*, covering topics such as our sexual impulse, love and pain, and sexual selection. By 1906, he was up to volume five, on sexual symbolism and why we find certain things and body parts hot. Finally, he was ready to tackle feet.

More than half of that volume is devoted to erotic symbolism, which is the term Ellis used for a desire for something that stands in for the whole body or person. Feet and shoes take up an entire section because Ellis found them almost everywhere he looked during his sex research. He wrote, "It would seem that even for the normal lover the foot is one of the most attractive parts of the body."

Ellis's work on feet was extensive, not least because he combined contemporary testimonies that he collected with stories from history and literature, such as Casanova in the eighteenth century and ancient China from thousands of years before his own time. He quoted from archives, journals, and the jaunty passages of Restif de la Bretonne, the French writer who developed the Cinderella story in 1769. Ellis does a fair amount of work thinking through Restif's fetishism for young women's feet and shoes, and is careful to point out that it was one example showing that masochism wasn't always involved. Ellis says, "[Restif] happened to see a pretty pair of shoes in a bootmaker's shop, and on hearing that they belonged to a girl whom at that time he reverently adored at a distance he blushed and nearly fainted." Sometimes a foot fetishist is pretty simple.

It was in Ellis's original case studies that the engine of his work settled into high gear. "AN" was twenty-nine, unmarried and healthy, "though not robust". It was a mystery how, but AN said he had reason to believe that his brother was an invert, or a man who fancied men. AN started to wear his dad's boots when he was six, and has loved men's boots and feet ever since. "A soldier in boots and spurs, a groom in tops, or even an errand-boy in patent leather leggings, fascinated me, and to this day, despite reason and everything else. The sight of such things produced an erection. An emission I could always produce by tightly tying my legs together." Ellis reported that AN was no woman hater, but that he clearly did not want to have sex with a woman. He found sodomy repulsive but also said he wasn't against it, as long as the other partner considered playing the "passive part".

In the case of "CP", Ellis found masochism at play. He described CP's desires to be focused on gratifying a sexual impulse more than exploring an interest in the other person. Specifically, he was a masochist who had substituted feet for a vulva, and trampling for sex. "When

38

I encounter a woman who very strongly attracts me and whom I very greatly admire," CP told Ellis, "my desire is never that I may have sexual connection with her in the ordinary sense, but that I may lie down upon the floor on my back and be trampled upon by her."

He liked his woman to be richly dressed, in an evening gown, with dainty high-heeled slippers, open just enough to show the in-step. He wanted her skirts to be raised, showing a liberal amount of ankle, but nothing above the knee because there is nothing there to interest him. CP even went so far as to say that nude women repelled him, something true for many foot fetishists that Freud would later overlook in his rush to draw a unifying theory around them. "The treading should be inflicted for a few minutes all over the chest, abdomen and groin, and lastly on the penis, which is, of course, lying along the belly in a violent state of erection, and consequently too hard for the treading to damage it. I also enjoy being nearly strangled by a woman's foot." If she wore high heels as she pressed down on his penis, he'd be visited by an "emission" that was an "agony of delight".

CP's testimony invites the modern-day reader to picture him, a well-to-do middle-aged man who was well known to Ellis. Maybe a doctor who worked in the hospital where Ellis had started to train as a physician. Or maybe he bunked in the same building in Paddington where Ellis lived in a bachelor pad, even after marrying

Edith Lees, a writer and proponent of women's rights. Lees was openly bisexual, and they lived in an open marriage. Ellis was known to be someone who didn't have much sex, at least not until he discovered later in life that he was really turned on by the sight of a woman having a wee. He wrote about all this in his autobiography from 1940, *My Life*.

Ellis is a curious man. I'm fascinated by how he met so many people who told him their darkest sexual fantasies and practices: clearly he and CP were good enough acquaintances that CP told him one that helped him to form a central part of his theory on sexuality. When CP was fourteen, around the 1870-80s, a family friend stood on him as a joke while she reached for a bangle from the mantelpiece. CP took her foot, kissed it, placed it on his hard penis – and immediately had an orgasm, "thoroughly and effectively". This apparently pleased the young woman, who was six years older than him, and they met many times to repeat the act. CP was sure that she had orgasms too.

Ellis clearly loved this story – he devoted a lot of time writing it down in his book. It joined similar stories in constructing Ellis's claims, where inversion (or homosexuality) is so fundamentally ingrained in a person's constitution that it battles through all the influences that try to make a person straight – an early version of "born this way". He believed a similar thing about foot fetishes, but more specifically said they were usually activated by one event, such as an "accidental association", that they "can usually, though not always, be traced to a definite starting point in the shock of some sexually emotional episode in early life".

This is a curious way of thinking about our fetish for feet. It recognises that our desires can be innate and also influenced by what's going on around us. So far, so good. But the very act of studying our fetishes as distinct and different implies that they are less pure than other desires.

Ellis and Krafft-Ebing set us on a path of sex that eventually requires a book like this one – an exploration of how we came to see our fetish for feet as weird. The work of those Victorian beard-strokers underpins the ways that we came to view foot fetishists. As a historian of sex, it's unsatisfying that the work of these men is all I have; we mustn't make the assumption that their findings offer the right way to think about sex and fetishes in the past. Instead we can actually use them to see how people decided to treat a fetish for feet. Krafft-Ebing said we are perverse. Ellis clarified that a fetish for feet was all part of the human experience, but his presentation characterised it as freakish. These ideas set us up in the twentieth century to look on people with this kink, as outsiders, deceitful, and weird.

Ever since the beard-strokers, storytellers have used their received wisdom to create characters who they want to rile their audience with. Fans of fantasy TV show *House of the Dragon* and its predecessor, *Game of Thrones*, are used to seeing incest, rape and beheading. But it was a character who revealed himself as having a foot fetish who viewers found "disgusting" and left them "scandalised" when it was first aired in October 2022.[28] In the scene, a man called Larys offers to tell Queen Alicent about the spies who are plotting against her – but only if she'll bare her feet for him. She reluctantly agrees, and Larys stares at her feet and wanks while sharing his intel. Cue the memes! Viewers posted pics of cartoon characters with their eyes burnt out, jokes about Larys being an OnlyFans subscriber, and lines such as "I can excuse incest, but I draw the line at foot fetish." Even the director of the episode, Clare Kilner, described Larys's wank as "really dirty". [29]

News stories about sex offenders often sensationalise a case involving feet: in one example from 2019, a man in a cinema in Leeds climbed under the seats to sexually assault two girls; what was 'worse' – and the lead fact in the news story – was that he was focused on their feet: "Foot fetish pervert climbed under seats at Leeds cinema and sexually assaulted girls", screamed the *Yorkshire Evening Post*.[30] This is classic tabloid reporting, dividing lines between what's normal and what isn't. The man was already an abuser, but the headline leading with his fetish would make him into a monster. I do not want to apologise for him or diminish his crime, but it is worth reflecting on why the specifics of it make it so much worse for involving feet. There is a pattern: crime news about similar abusers always places their fetish for feet at the top, maximising the scandal and the crime.

It's also really common for a person to imply that they are normal because they are not a foot fetishist. James Gunn, who directs Hollywood superhero movies including *The Suicide Squad* starring Margot Robbie, had to process why moviegoers loved the scene where she grabs some keys with her toes more than the bombs and collapsing buildings. "I don't know where these people come from," Gunn joked, speaking on *Jimmy Kimmel Live* in 2021.[31] "'Do we get to see Margot's feet?' I'm like, *That's what you're thinking about?*"

In 2022, Jen Metcalfe, an actor in TV soap *Hollyoaks* gave an exclusive interview to a tabloid newspaper to say that the only people sliding into her DMs were "weird foot fetish guys".[32] In case you had any doubt about these guys, she added, "There are definitely no eligible bachelors, let's put it that way."

This idea that a person is unusual or dirty if they have a foot fetish is grounded in the nineteenth century. When you read through the early sexology, you find a fetish for feet everywhere – plus the novel idea that it was a perversion. Previously, an interest in feet had been an open part of culture, and even rhapsodised about.

The idea that it should be a perversion was invented by powerful men with big beards and big egos. They discovered just how widespread foot fetishism is, and they laid down ways of thinking about it more than a hundred years ago that still stick to us today. That is why it is not just common, but also acceptable, to villainise or mock someone who fancies feet. Ellis was right to observe this kink as part of the human experience, but his and others' desire to treat it as unusual has had a lasting cultural and social impact. The ideas of the Victorian and Edwardian scientists have lived on in all of us far longer than they deserved to.

They were not the last beard-strokers to taint our fetish for feet, because as time rolled into the twentieth century, a new type of scientist got involved. They wanted to understand *why*. And to do this they would have to poke around in the darkest corners of our thoughts.

Chapter 3
A Particular and Quite Special Penis

When I started to look into our fetish for feet, somehow I knew deep down that Sigmund Freud would turn up: surely the daddy of psychoanalysis would have something to say about it.

Writing around the same time as Ellis was investigating foot fetishes, in the first of his *Three Essays on the Theory of Sexuality* from 1905, Freud said of fetishism, "No other variation of the sexual instinct that borders on the pathological can lay so much claim to our interest as this one".[33]

He saw fetish as abnormal, continuing the Victorian lineage in describing fetishism as wonky in one way or another, an "unsuitable substitute" for a normal sexual object. He wrote that a foot is "very inappropriate for sexual purposes", revealing a pretty narrow idea of what sex could be. He suggests a few reasons for a fetish, from "executive weakness of the sexual apparatus" leading to a mistargeted desire to abandonment of desire altogether. A fetish is "pathological", Freud said, when it completely subsumes the other, more 'normal' sexual desires.

With that word he continued to use a harmful way of thinking about fetishes that the sexologists had created. It's funny now, when you read Freud, or any of these early beard-strokers. They're using scientific language where there is no science, to grasp for solutions to a problem that doesn't exist, and somehow coming up with ways of thinking that have stuck to people like me.

In order to stay true to the facts of the full breadth of sexual interests that had been observed in people, Freud had to separate sexual practices from gender (acknowledging, for example, that a person's sexuality does not derive from whether they are a man or a woman). This insight remains with us, but in his essay in 1905 it was a radical way to think about sex.

In 1914, he gave a talk to the Vienna Psycho-Analytical Society about a case of foot fetishism, wondering aloud whether men fancied women's feet because they were imagining approaching her genitals from below. He later said that men who found eroticism in velvet and fur were really fixated on the idea of women's pubic hair. Freud obsessively claimed that a fetish always had a genital connection.

By 1927, he was ready to go deep into fetishes. He had been hearing from a number of men with different fetishes, including one who fancied noses so much that he saw them as shining at him as he skipped through life. After hearing such cases (including plenty concerning feet), Freud published a paper simply called "Fetishism"[34]. In this essay he wanted to spend some time thinking through why people had fetishises, including the paradox that they were so commonplace and yet 'abnormal' in the way that he thought sexual desire developed. Freud's idea that heterosexual men developed their sexuality through an early desire for their mother was well developed by this point. This 'Oedipal theory', named after the character Oedipus Rex in an ancient play by Sophocles, held that little boys resent their fathers for having access to their mothers; but as they mature sexually they see their fathers less as a rival and more as a role model, and thus come to desire women, like their father desired their mother. In writing "Fetishism", Freud wanted to know how desires like foot fancying could fit into this theory.

"When now I announce that the fetish is a substitute for the penis, I shall certainly create disappointment," he wrote, "so I hasten to add that it is not a substitute for any chance penis, but for a particular and quite special penis that had been extremely important in early childhood but had later been lost."

Freud's particular and quite special penis is also unsurprising: it is the one that every little boy thinks his mother has, until he realises that she does not. The little boy who grows up to have a fetish does not want to give up the dream of his mum's dick, so his unconscious self creates one for her, in the future women he fancies, in the form of her feet, hair, navel, or nose. Thinking about fetishes enabled Freud to persist with his idea that the sexuality of men is grounded in their reactions to noticing that their mothers don't have a penis like they do – giving them the fear that their penis might be removed (castration anxiety). In his essay on fetishism, though, he had to admit that fetishists and homosexuals didn't fit his models, and so he couldn't explain them. "Probably no male human being is spared the fright of castration at the sight of a female genital," wrote Freud, deadpan. "Why some people become homosexual as a consequence of that impression, while others fend it off by creating a fetish, and the great majority surmount it, we are frankly not able to explain."

It's remarkable that Freud's theories managed to benefit from the gloss of science while at the same time sidestepping the requirement that science places on theories, which is that they be demonstrable. He read Ellis, who found cases of men who fancied women's feet but not their vulvas, and kept going with the idea that a foot fetish was always ultimately linked to genitals.

Other fetishes he discussed in his essay include those for underwear and women's fabrics, probably because they can more easily fit into his suggestion that it's all ultimately linked to wanting to have sex with a woman. As he says himself, it hard to guess how gays fit into the picture. And yet, there we were, sniffing men's boots in front of Ellis and his notepad.

Thinking about fetishism gave Freud another opportunity to reflect on his broader ideas. He wrote that a male who sees female genitals still hopes on some level that she might have a penis, writing, "He retains this belief but he also gives it up." A male foot fetishist manages to get turned on by a woman's foot because he accepts it as a substitute for the penis that the woman doesn't have – but at the same time he still needs to believe that the foot is a penis, in order for the attraction to work. I'm sure you're laughing as you read this. But Freud was dead serious about this idea, and by this point in his career he'd been accepted as an influence and an authority because of his theories. The psychoanalytical profession as a whole had largely been accepted as a science, too.

It's hard to know what Freud would have made of me: I want the man's foot but I also want his dick. His foot isn't a dick to me, because I can enjoy his actual dick too. Girl, so confusing.

Many of Freud's ideas have fallen out of favour with psychoanalysts, therapists and psychologists today. Yet they remain as a foundation for the idea that sexuality is not solely a biological construct, and that it is shaped as we develop and interact with others. He also insisted that most people are not 'normal', which also remains a useful idea. A statue of Freud still squats outside the Tavistock Centre in London, the UK's foremost centre for mental health research and treatment. His texts remain on the reading lists of trainees in the psychological fields. According to the global database of scientific papers published across the more than 4,000 journals owned by the publishing company Elsevier, from 2011 to 2021, every working day researchers and clinicians published a new paper mentioning Sigmund Freud. His ideas about sex and fetishism, as explored in his "Three Essays" and "Fetishism", continued to shape how we think of ourselves a century later.

There is one more key beard-stroker worth mentioning in the tour through how foot fetishism became a perversion. It is a man named Wilhelm Stekel, who was born in 1868 in Boiany in what is now Ukraine but was then an eastern province of the Austro-Hungarian empire. Young Stekel was originally apprenticed to a shoemaker, but never mentioned this in an account of a boot fetishist that he recorded much later, when he was a psychoanalyst. Stekel had also done military service, which he hated. So, you have to wonder what was on *his* mind when a patient he called Mr Beta told him about his obsession with soldiers' boots and their swollen, sweaty, bloody feet.

Published in 1930, Stekel's book *Sexual Aberrations: The Phenomena of Fetishism in Relation to Sex* was an extensive study covering a range of sexual fetishes, from hands to wigs to aprons, and also delves into incest and kleptomania. He wrote a whole chapter devoted to the case of one man "suffering" from a foot fetish. That man was Mr Beta.[35] According to Stekel's account, Mr Beta did a lot of dashing around as a result of his obsession: "He raves about feet and feels impelled to run after persons with feet of the shape he delights to see," he wrote. "He could go through the streets for hours in this wise and loved best to go for the Danube where there are often numbers of men who pull off their shoes, unwrap the rags from their feet and lie down to sun themselves or cool their feet in the river... It is the sight of these large, red feet which then gives him a thrill. He rushes home to masturbate."

The more swollen, red and sweaty those feet, the better. Stekel investigated Mr Beta's desire for more than a year, and went deeper and deeper into his past and his identity in over fifty pages of detail. Mr Beta loved the feet of labourers – hence the working men by the river, soothing their tired soles. He remembered that when he was a child a soldier visited his family home, and pulled off his boots in the kitchen revealing big red feet. The soldier rocked little Mr Beta on his lap, which gave the embryonic foot fiend a "rush of pleasure in his veins", according to Stekel.

Mr Beta told Stekel all about his family life: his mother died in childbirth, his dad and the governess became lovers, which made Mr Beta hate the governess at the same time that he found himself fascinated with his dad's feet. He used to suck his big toe as a child. He respected his dad, and when his dad told him about sex and the chance of venereal disease, Mr Beta vowed not to disappoint him – so he avoided sex altogether. He even waited three years until after his dad had died before doing it. But he found sex difficult, often losing his erection, scared that his penis would get stuck in the woman's vagina and he would lose it. "He would be caught in the caverns of the mother's body and wouldn't be able to escape…"

Beyond these nightmares, Mr Beta also talked about his dreams. There is a lot of killing, an intense rivalry with the English governess, and a wooden image of Christ that Beta took a piece from. The final analysis from Stekel was that Mr Beta felt guilty towards his mum, based on a morbid belief that his own big toe had lodged itself inside her as he was being born, causing her death. "He desired to castrate his father for having had intercourse with the Englishwoman," Stekel reported. "Then he wants to emasculate himself. The piece that he wants to take from himself (see the dream of the wooden image) is the genital. Then he can become Christ. He is the criminal, the mother killer who is innocent of the crime."

"The result was a displacement of all his erotic libido to the foot," says Stekel. And then back to the mum, and the dreams: Stekel noticed that Mr Beta really liked damaged feet, especially bloody ones. "He would often fantasy [sic] that he had stuck a nail or splinter into his foot and that it bled. The picture of a foot with a nail in it appeared more and more frequently in his fantasies and day-dreams. In short, there appeared that phenomenon which I have found so often in parapathics: the Christ neurosis."

'Neurosis' is a broad and fairly generic term for emotional distress. Stekel said that Mr Beta's neurosis was grounded in Christ, and led to his foot fetish. His erotic fascination with feet ensured his chastity (no penis involved!), and because it was related to Christ's suffering, it would mean he could overcome the guilt at killing his mum, be admitted into heaven, and reach sainthood. This leads to a sentence of Stekel's that must be one of the greatest uses of punctuation in a century and a half of sexology: "His God was—the foot."

So, to recap what the various beard-strokers thought: male foot fetishists' desires are perverse, abnormal, confused, filled with hate, and even the result of something called 'Christ neurosis'. Even when their intention was to study fetishes for the sake of improving our understanding of our desires, the result is that they left behind the idea that a foot fetish is weird. And, worse, wrong.

The acts of the early sexologists in particular were to collect stories from fetishists, make them legends, and pathologise them, argued Emily Apter, a researcher who has studied the history of psychoanalysis. "They were built up as medical dossiers and collected like so many rare specimens," she wrote of men like Freud in her book *Feminising the Fetish* from 1991. "Each case study was exhibited, as in a psychohistorical museum, demonstrating individually the determinative traits of a govern perversion, obsession, or paranormal idée fixe, and exemplifying as a totality the taxonomy of criminal anomaly."[36]

This is allied to how those working in the psychological fields have treated homosexuality which, in the middle of the twentieth century, became the number one menace that their profession sought to stamp out.

Psychoanalysis and psychiatry monopolised how to think about sadomasochism, fetishes, and homosexuality. They developed the work of sexologists, but still rooted our desires in pathology – an illness awaiting a cure, or a deviance needing containment. This had real, harmful effects.

In the USA in 1952, the American Psychiatric Association listed homosexuality and 'sexual sadism', a term which has long included fetishes such as feet, as sociopathic personality disturbances in its first edition of the *Diagnostic and Statistical Manual of Mental Disorders*. This set the standards for the whole profession of what symptoms are classified as deviant and resulting in specific mental health conditions. 'Sexual masochism' was added in 1968, defined in later editions as enjoying acts featuring humiliation and suffering. Homosexuality remained classed as a sociopathic disorder until 1973, when it was revised from a 'deviance' into a 'disturbance'. In still later editions, up to 2013, it was described as a sexual disorder. Variations on sadism and masochism, and other paraphilias (broadly, fetishes) such as exhibitionism appeared in subsequent editions. It wasn't until 2013 when the then new edition, *DSM-5*, stated that "a paraphilia by itself does not necessarily justify or require clinical intervention".

Although this seemed to imply that fetishes might be normal by default, our kinks remained pathologised. There did come an acknowledgement that we may find pleasure in them; the International Classification of Diseases used by the United Nations further removed fetishism and sadomasochism as mental illnesses in 2019. Still, paraphilias remain in the *DSM* and fetishes culturally are still seen as unusual. This shows how the ideas of early sexologists from the Victorian and Edwardian periods remained so powerful. They pathologised our fetishes and other sexual practices that sat outside of the image of a man penetrating a reclining woman. They used language and classifications that are still believed by some lawmakers, doctors, religious leaders and mental health professionals in many countries. They are the reason why into the 1990s and 2000s psychotherapists were still debating whether they would allow gays and lesbians to join their profession. And why some people who had managed to train as psychoanalysts were, in 2019, still detecting among their ranks "undercurrents of homophobia and casual cruelty towards those whose gender and sexuality do not 'fit' with the heteronormativity that some describe as 'natural',"[37] according to Leezah Hertzmann and Juliet Newbigin, the editors of a book called *Sexuality and Gender Now Moving Beyond Heteronormativity.*

It didn't matter how much the psychological fields distanced themselves from the beard-strokers, they have lingered. "The relics of deviance, perversion and paraphilias still permeate theory and practice in psychotherapy today," said psychotherapist Amanda Middleton in an interview with Jane C. Czyzselska for the latter's book *Queering Psychotherapy.* "That has a detrimental effect on people's well-being in everyday life."[38]

Middleton, Czyzselska, Hertzmann and Newbigin know that the prejudices they were trying to get therapy colleagues to recognise stem partly from the work of their professional ancestors in psychiatry and sexology. "Therapists, myself included, must think about how to ensure we aren't doing harm to clients, harm that comes directly from our ideas and theories and their impact on marginalised genders, sexualities and forms of relationship," said Middleton. "There's a real risk right now of therapists repeating harmful patterns from the past."

These harmful patterns have perpetuated in other fields, too: laws around the world empower police to arrest people for having same-sex relationships, and judges to convict them; trans people are denied basic healthcare and vilified; and dangerous shitbags still skip around offering spurious, legally protected 'conversion therapies'.

The roots of so many of this gender- and sexuality-based violence lie in early psychology, in the hands of the beard-strokers.

"Psychologists and psychiatrists have been telling us what's normal and what isn't for a very long time," wrote Justin Lehmiller in *Tell Me What You Want*. "Basically, whenever they've encountered something that doesn't appear normal to them, they have erred on the side of calling it a paraphilia, even in the absence of evidence that a given desire is rare or unusual. This freewheeling, arbitrary tendency to label desire after desire as paraphilic has had the problematic effect of stigmatising far too many sexual interests because, for almost the entire time the *DSM* has been in existence, the term paraphilia has been synonymous with mental disorder."

How did this happen? I think a lot of it comes down to the time and places where sexology began, as seen in the work of Krafft-Ebing and Ellis. There was a group of people, almost all men, and all white, all from the middle and upper classes, living in imperial nations such as England and Germany, that were industrialising rapidly in the nineteenth century thanks to advances in science and technology. All these factors placed these men onto a platform of supreme confidence, power, influence and the belief that science and rationality were the driving forces behind a modern society. The result was that they studied people's desires with the same attention that a microbiologist uses to examine bacteria, or an engineer uses when measuring the correct angle for a suspension bridge. They attempted to be objective, when they were anything but. From their assumption that the way they lived was right – or the way that members of their class claimed was right – they made judgements about what was normal, what was perverse, and what must be a problem. In fact, Ellis was an active eugenicist who believed in different races among people, and a hierarchy between them.

And, in the case of Freud and Stekel and similar psychoanalytical thinkers, they made up theories to tie together the stories that people told about their desires. Through all this work on sex, fetishes in particular became a dividing line between what was normal and what was not. Even the amount of time and energy spent through the generations on analysing fetishists might have given our desires more weight than they're really worth.

You may think that I'm implying that we should stop studying our desires. I don't think that. It's important to talk and think and write about sex, of course. Research from mental health professionals and social scientists about what makes us tick is so useful, not least for showing us how freaky most of us are, even if it's impossible to land on the perfect methodology for cracking into our deepest desires. I believe we all need to be talking and thinking more about sex. In order for all that to happen, perhaps it has been useful for us to go through the judge-mental categorisation and the silly theorising. This is a paradox that we may have to live with.

But we do also have to live with the poison that these people and thinkers have put inside us. Although our attitudes towards sex, and specifically fetishes, have changed since people began to pathologise us, many of us still experience what happened one night to Mark, the man with drawers and drawers of used socks bought online. He was in a sex club and he saw a guy who looked hot, wearing a suit with black socks. "I just said to him, you know, could I have a feel of your socks and your feet?" The guy did not just say no thanks. He said, "That's fucking weird", and walked off. Mark was left alone, standing in his shame.

Reed had similar experiences when she tried to explore a fetish for feet. She worked on the kind of TV channel where women pose for the camera and men watching at home text or call them. The sex workers like Reed had to fit into regulated norms of what could be shown on television and the related social media channels (no bare tits, ass or genitals), and so she found herself sometimes posing with her feet. This was unusual. Her colleagues usually avoided calls from guys who wanted to talk about their feet. And they disapproved of Reed showing her own feet on camera. "A lot of the girls rejected me for that," she said. "Not only was I being shamed, enjoying feet myself and giving foot massages for the camera, but also I was now treated like one of the 'perverted, gross guys'."

Reed managed to turn this shame upside down. First, the money and respect she got from those guys was often better than from other calls. Then she found the pleasure in playing with her feet, and finding other people to play along too. It is possible to dilute the poison put inside us all. These beard-strokers made people like Reed, Mark and me into perverts even before we were born. They wrote the script for the man who told Mark he was "fucking weird". And they lived rent-free in my head as inner cops, telling me I was wrong for liking feet.

Even as they made affirming and useful insights, the beard-strokers did untold damage to us. Instead of opening up our sexual imaginations, their descriptions, categorisations and guesses closed them down. Therapists who ground their work in queer politics and kink-positivity have changed this course of history for the better. But it is the artists and performers who offer the most exciting insights into our fetish for feet.

Chapter 4
OnlyFeet

When a Frenchman named Pierre Molinier died in 1976, he left behind hundreds of beautiful, bizarre images. His photographs are dark, funny, surprising, and intensely erotic. They often feature human legs, almost always in stockings. Usually they belong to Pierre himself. His athletic and slender legs kick and flail. Sometimes they stand tall on high heels, strong enough to hold up the world.

In one photo he reclines on a chaise lounge. His feet have taken to the air in laced-up heels. He has done some planning for this photo. He set up the camera and laid the cable with a remote control button for the shutter release. He positioned himself as he wanted to be seen, and so that he could take the photo when it pleased him. He also augmented one of his high heels by attaching a dildo. It is with this heel/dildo – and the strength and angle of his stockinged leg – that Pierre is fucking himself. If you look closely at this black and white image, although most of his face is concealed, you can see that he is smiling.

Pierre's photos look older than they are. They could be snaps from a secret society in the nineteenth century. But they are also a record from the future: a time when we are able to manifest our desires. If Pierre could do it, perhaps I can, too. Instead, he was working in the middle of the twentieth century, in a Catholic country divided into genders and sexualities. His art is remarkable for this: he ignored conventions and expectations, and he made his desires come to life. He loved high heels so much that he penetrated himself with one. What's more: he performed that sex act for the world. Through his erotic art, Pierre looks directly at the viewer and says *This is my freak, what's yours?*

That question is what makes his work special and, in my opinion, good art. It is provocative in the erotic way, it forces a reaction, and it places feet in the frame. Pierre's photography is beautiful. It is the kind of beauty that might not be aesthetically pleasing to everyone; it is beautiful because you know it to be true and honest. Many of us whose desire includes feet do not admit that fully to ourselves, but Pierre went all the way and made sexy pics about it. In fact, history is filled with artists and makers who have been attracted to the foot enough to represent it. Often this is incidental, as in the case of Michelangelo who carved David's feet in marble and made a fine sculpture. But often feet are the star of the show, like Pierre's, and it is worth spending time with them. The thing about people who *focus* on representing feet is that they are variously a mix of artists, sex workers, fetishists, thinkers and lovers. People like Pierre can reveal far more about how we feel about feet than those who study it from outside.

Foot fetish art is a riposte to the legacies of the beard-strokers, but it is also so much more – it is the truer treatment of our interest in feet than science, or pseudo-science, could ever manage. As foot fetishist Tina Horn wrote, "I feel a camaraderie with someone who sees feet the way I do: as characters."[39] In saying that, Horn was humanising a body part that is so often villainised. She was right to read the detail in our feet and infer personality. I love that. It is a sensibility that runs through the work of another erotic photographer, Elmer Batters.

When he was in the US Navy, Batters realised that he was different to the other sailors who fancied women. They were into tits and ass, but he was into legs and feet. Discharged after World War Two, Batters began to take photos of women in stockings. He worked through the artistic boom of the 1960s and '70s but felt ostracised by the art world because of his subject. He kept going, producing enticing and often funny photographs. They are erotic, kinky, sexy and shamelessly, happily fetishistic.

Some of them feature women licking each other's toes; others place elegant stockinged feet on the dashboards of classic cars. Batters sold much of his work to kinky magazines, such as *Leg Show*, which was published in the USA in the 1980s and '90s, and depicted dominant women in nylons, corsets, pantyhose, stockings and high heels. Publishing in *Leg Show* helped Batters to bridge art photography and porn. The editor of *Leg Show*, Dian Hanson, commissioned Batters' work from 1986 until his death in 1997. "He'd tell people he made this photography because his publishers asked for it, not because he was into it himself," Hanson told Madeleine Pollard, for Elephant Art.[40]

Gay and queer fetish artists have been less coy. If your sexuality is already perceived as unusual, you don't lose much else by showing that it's kinky too. Perhaps that is all a viewer is able to know. "I don't think that by looking at my drawings that they would be able to tell much about my personality," said the foot fetish artist known as Etienne, in an interview for the National Gay Art Archives in 1983.[41] "However, an observer could probably pick up on a lot of surface things like, 'wow, he's into white sox'."

Etienne's drawings and paintings showed off sumptuous male bodies, with bulging muscles and square jawlines. Often his compositions featured feet, with a clear fetishistic focus – usually the subjects' feet were sheathed in leather boots or steaming socks. Some of these characters featured as murals, painted by Etienne on the walls of the first bar in the world to cater to men into leather. The Gold Coast bar was founded by Etienne and his partner in Chicago in 1958. The bar quickly became a space for kinky men to meet. And this included the foot freaks who enjoyed Etienne's drawings of hunks. I was struck by something the artist said in 1983 when he was asked about what people might take from his art. "I think it would be nice if they would find it exuberant," he said, "that there is life in it, that it would sound echoes of a nice spirit."

I would say that yes, there is life in Etienne's art, but also in his community work: building a space for people who wanted to explore sexual pleasure together. This is simply another way of manifesting our fetish for feet – by facilitating people to actually play with their desires. But it also makes me think about the way our lives are divided strictly. Etienne helped to create a public space and made very public art. Batters remained coy about his private desires, but he put his name to the photographs he published in porn magazines. And Pierre Molinier seemed to imbue his art with secrecy. When you look at his pictures you feel like you are peeping into his boudoir through a keyhole, and if you enter and give into the pleasures there you will remain sealed off from the bustling, polluted street outside. I think this secrecy

– or perhaps privacy – is one of the qualities of Pierre's work that is most successful. It does not imply shame, but rather a commitment to his own desires.

This devotion struck Ajamu when he first saw Pierre's photos, in London's Cabinet Gallery in 1993, when it was based in Brixton. It was only a year after Ajamu had started playing with a lover's feet, and all of a sudden here was Pierre in his stockings and dildo-heel. Walking around that exhibition, Ajamu "was drawn to the idea that his work was made for himself, and for his own pleasure." As someone with an interest in feet, heels and stockings, Ajamu was pulled into Pierre's world. It is a completely different world to the bar that Etienne co-founded; this world exists in his own fantasy, really, and that is partly because his art was made in the private space of a studio (or boudoir).

"It was just meant for him," said Ajamu, seated on a stool across from me. I was visiting him in his own studio, which he constructed some time after seeing Pierre's pictures. Ajamu filled his private space with lighting rigs, black fabric, books, contact sheets and cameras. Inspired by Pierre, and his own desires, Ajamu became Ajamu X, an extraordinary darkroom/fine art photographic artist.

Many of Ajamu X's greatest photographs explore his fetish for feet, in exquisite black-and-white clarity. There are men's feet held aloft, sometimes by a lover, and capped by shoes with heels made from drill bits. There is Master

Aab, seated on a grand chair and wearing lace gloves, holding a chain around the neck of his submissive, who is being used as a footstool for the master's majestic soles. And there is the artist himself, a self-portrait where his own feet fill the frame, and another where he reclines on a chaise lounge, in a leather mask, stockings and heels. A review of the exhibition that inspired Ajamu in 1993 argued: "Pierre Molinier lived the violence and sexual obsessions his fellow Surrealists only dreamt about. Now barely remembered as a footnote to the Surrealist movement, it was Molinier – not Dali, nor Magritte – who did it for real."[42]

Long after Pierre died, Ajamu X continued doing it for real. Ajamu X's art celebrates and explores many other body parts, but it is clear that feet are on his menu. He makes the reader think about pleasure by playing with assumptions that limit us, such as 'stockings are only for women' and 'men who are racialised as Black can't be sexually tender, together'. Feet are so demonised in society in general that they offer Ajamu X a shortcut into provoking a reaction. When he casts a foot as a thing of beauty, because of how it is lit and shot, and how it is implicated in sensuality, he blows minds wide open. "People still also associate feet with dirt," he told me. "Feet are seen as either smelly, or need to be washed or covered over. People cannot get their head around the idea that this thing can also be pleasurable."

This is a classic thing said by fetishists, and in fact anyone with a sexual desire that is seen as unusual. It's also how Dug felt, growing up in the midwest in the generation born after World War Two, knowing that his interest in feet was not fully accepted. "I felt so out of place," he told me. This didn't stop him exploring it, and as a young man he began taking photographs and making videos. They usually featured him 'worshipping' the feet of straight, masculine men. The people in Dug's work remained clothed, and they never played with dicks or bums. They didn't even kiss on the lips. Dug's focus was feet – and Dug discovered that people really liked that. Through the 1970s, '80s and '90s he found guys through gay magazines such as *Drummer* and *The Advocate*, and he built the Foot Fraternity. This club is the home of four million images and more than 10,000 films. It is an enormous community of people who love feet. At the heart of the network is Dug, a very humble man in a house in a suburb of Cleveland, Ohio. Dug Gaines started as a fetishist, but became something extraordinary: an artist, collector, publisher, and community leader.

"I didn't feel like I brought them here," he told me. "It wasn't me… They need[ed] to be here to find their own kind, and identify with others who feel as they did."

The Foot Fraternity sits in a long line of clubs for foot fetishists. As a Londoner, I'm familiar with Club Pedestal, a long-running club night for submissive men and dominant women, often with a focus on foot worship; and Feet on Friday which runs a monthly foot night for men in the basement of Central Station, a friendly gay pub. Before these, London was home to The Palace of Pedic Pleasure. "The place was furnished in good though not lavish taste," wrote William A. Rossi in 1976, about his visit to the 'palace', some years before. "Several men and women, fully clothed, were sitting around talking and drinking. But soon, some of the men, paired with their selected women, disappeared."[43]

Rossi reported how the madam called her clients "sexual sophisticates" who visited from all over Britain and other European countries, and even the USA. "Our girls are very special," said the madam, adding that they were all taught in the art of "pedic lovemaking". Dug's Foot Fraternity has been mostly virtual – essentially a mail order business, with money and photos sent through the post, and men meeting each other via adverts. Later, it took advantage of the internet for instant connection and sales. The Foot Fraternity is not a party or a brothel and, Dug insisted to me, its photographic output is not even pornography.

"My work has been sensual erotica," he told me. "There is no nudity… My work has never been porn, right? You don't need it."

(Speak for yourself, Dug!)

Occasionally members request videos or photos of the models getting naked and having oral or anal penetration, but Dug says he's never made them. "I'm sorry, but... I'm not comfortable doing nudity." Instead, he tells members to watch the videos of one man licking another's feet and to look at their bulge if they want to. "Your imagination could fill in," he said. I think that although there might be part of Dug that thinks porn isn't classy, his creative policy is more driven by his own actual desire, like Pierre's. The fact is that Dug is a pure foot fetishist: worshipping feet is the only sex act he's interested in. He once had a partner, but they switched to being friends instead. "I was cheating him because what I liked centrally [and] what he likes centrally were different," he told me. "We couldn't live together as lovers."

Dug's intense focus on feet shows up in the billions of pixels he has produced, catalogued, published and distributed – and the thousands of fetishists he has brought together. It is an extraordinary achievement, grounded in the love and respect he has for himself and other fetishists.

Although Dug prefers to avoid the category of 'pornography', the filmmaker Erika Lust embraced it. Lust makes porn films featuring all sorts of different bodies, desires and kinks. In 2014, she angled her lens down towards feet, in a film entitled *Do You Find My Feet Suckable?*, where a man and a woman in a library abandon their studies to indulge in some foot play. Lust made another foot fetish film in 2018, entitled *Dirty Feet*, featuring two real-life partners, Lucy and Miro, savouring each other's toes while playing around in mud. In 2022, Lust spoke about why feet caught her creative imagination:

> We accumulate a lot of tension in our feet since they're covered with nerve endings, so massaging them can be almost orgasmic by itself at times... Foot kissing and toe sucking are also considered very erotic by many, and I guess their component of supposed 'dirtiness' might be among the aspects that make them more arousing.[44]

As an artist, Lust, too, plays around with how many people view feet. The internet has provided an ever-expanding platform for our fetishes. In 2023, the online video site PornHub reported a 68% jump in searches for 'feet' among Generation Z.[45] It's still not always something people admit to, though – even online where it's possible to be anonymous. In data from Grindr from 2023, 'feet' appeared as one of the top five searched-for tags, but not in the top five tags that people chose to display on their own profile.[46]

On Instagram, X, and Tiktok, users post pictures and videos of their feet (also socks and shoes), spanning the breadth of style from mundane to artistic to pornographic, depending on the platform's rules. Tags range from #FootWorship to #SuckableToes, and content piles up by the terabyte. People meet on Reddit to share what tags to use for the other platforms, and discuss their favourite videos. Sometimes it seems like everyone is doing it. Maybe everyone is an artist these days, although most don't have the elegance of Ajamu X or the shock factor of Pierre. The barrier to posting foot pics online is so low that the practice has flourished. There is no sexually explicit material allowed on Instagram or Tiktok, but feet are free to roam. Not classed as 'sex', content featuring socks, stockings and feet carve out a sizeable part of Instagram and Tiktok.

Mark's enormous collection of socks has been fulfilled by interacting with these amateurs. They post pics of their feet in socks, and he contacts them to buy the socks. He prefers the owners to be straight men, and to have worn the socks for some time, imbuing them with their sweat and stink. He spends up to £500 per month on used socks. Mark also runs his own foot fetish Instagram account, posting photos of his own feet in the socks he's bought online. "I have to be able to wear them," he told me, elaborating on his relationship with one seller, a sports teacher who has a girlfriend. "As soon as he takes them off, he puts them in plastic and seals them," says Mark, who sends him money and receives a muggy bag of socks a few days later. When Mark told me about this, I wondered: is this just another creative manifestation of our fetish for feet?

I decided not to go too far down the hole of figuring out whether the young man's sweaty socks are an artistic expression... because instead it made me also think about the commercialisation of our fetish for feet. The internet is a market: people sell used socks to fetishists via X and Vinted, and pics and videos on OnlyFans. Soon after the latter site launched in 2016, it became dominated by porn. By 2023, it had more than 3 million content creators and 220 million consumers.[47] The vast majority of the content is sex related, with accounts dedicated to sexy wrestling, people who sell their farts in jars, and all the various types of fucking you can imagine. When it comes to feet, content creators typically sell pics or videos, sometimes doing specific things like squashing grapes or using their feet to wank a penis. If you follow foot fetish news like I do, you'll notice a common story. It usually features a famous person who is making extra money by selling foot pics (before Lily Allen, the rapper and model Blac Chyna was up to it) or a regular person who makes a fortune doing it. A man from Arizona was raking in $4,000 a month in 2021, at the time of a *Mail Online* article that featured the glib headline "Selling his sole!"[48]

The subject of the article, Jason Stromm, has large feet and a muscly body. He plays a bit on his size in some of his photos and videos, encouraging his audience to enjoy the feeling that they are small compared to him. He sells his sweaty socks too. Stromm knows what his audience likes partly because he also has a fetish for feet, much like Reed. After years working for other people in the sex industry, Reed decided to sell her own content online. She told me in 2024 that around 10-15% of her income as a sex worker directly came from her OnlyFans account where she specialises in foot fetish content. Her videos show her being tickled or having a bath after a pedicure. As a performer she has listened to what her subscribers like. She discovered that men loved her prominent big toes. "And, of course, the nail colour," she said. "Nail colour can really sway a person from enjoying the foot." Some of her subscribers prefer her toes without any nail polish, and some like bright colours. "Whenever I put a poll up asking what colour do I change my toes to, the result is always black!"

The thing is, even if Reed served the bulk of her audience and only ever painted her toenails black, those who liked pink or scarlet or cerulean could find a creator on OnlyFans just for them. This is the nature of online porn: it divides into ever more niche desires, and even helps to create them. When Dug started sending out photos to people who answered his ads, there was a limit to how much personalisation he could achieve. Artists such as Pierre and Ajamu X only ever sought to externalise their own desires and reveal their own pleasures. OnlyFans is a wonderful explosion of human sexuality. I have found (and paid for) gorgeous content that gives me pleasure. I've even interacted directly with those who make it. Sometimes it feels that by finding a creator who matches our freaks, we are able to channel directly into our desires, and this is beautiful.

The best artists, including those who have created work that explores our fetish for feet, are the ones who unveil our unmitigated pleasures. Folks like Reed, Dug, Ajamu and Pierre Molinier have used their sexual and creative passions to pioneer new ways of imagining pleasure. They honour the long history of people playing with feet, while making their ripostes to those who called them perverts. They show how we all have sexual imaginations and the capacity to explore them. We can be the creator of our own desires. And that is why I now want to find the freak inside us all.

Conclusion
The Freak Inside

Usually we just bump into each other at raves. In the darkness you're weird and you're sexy. I'm happy I saw you here too, in the light of the garden outside my flat, among friends. I like to see you have a good time. The party has wound down and I'm glad you came.

You say you're leaving. But somehow we're in my bedroom and I'm kissing you. You give your tongue to me. At first it's like a thank you... then, something else. Now we're kissing each other. Touching. Breathing together. I'm pressing myself into you. We're grasping for each other's dicks like teenage gay boys.

Somehow I'm on the floor. I think I was pulling down your trackies? They're now discarded, and here I am with them, at your feet. You stare at me, breathing.

You find your moment, and you lift your socked foot, and you place it against my face. Your foot pushes me down.

My eyes look up, into yours.

We breathe.

When I started giving in to my fetish for feet, I found myself in moments like this. I allowed my body to melt into its pleasures. In fact, if I'm honest, finally I was pursuing something that had intrigued me since I was a child. I'd always known simply that I was interested in men's feet. Summer always came as a treat – sandal season! In films, tired characters sometimes propped up their dogs on the arm of a couch. Ads for holidays showed men going barefoot on the beach. I looked out for all of these, all the time. As Tina Horn wrote, "Fetish is an aesthetic of intrigue."[49]

Even touching and playing didn't satiate my interest. My intrigue went further than most: I needed to *know* more. This is what took me into history. My loved ones will tell you that in order for me to understand something, I have to make work out of it. So here I am, approaching the end of a long journey into the history of our fetish for feet.

I have read through piles of books and papers, watched a lot of videos including porn, absorbed artworks, slipped into basement sex clubs, and held countless conversations. It might be the interviews specifically with Ajamu, Dug, Reed and Mark that have most informed this book. I spoke to them because I wanted to explore different perspectives from my own and I couldn't speak to all the dead people from history. Those four people indulged my questions, trusted me with their stories, and – most importantly – they taught me something that I want to explore as the book comes to its end. If we can learn anything from a history of our fetish for feet, it is the power of pleasure.

This is what Ajamu X focuses his lens on. That much is obvious in his work, where pleasure often ripples through his human subjects. But what surprised me when I spoke to him was how much he draws on a history of pleasure. The man is obsessed with Pierre Molinier, one of his principal artistic ancestors. Feet are not central to their photography, but the way they both use feet – that is, the way they give into their own intrigue about feet – reveals so much about our bodies' potential for pleasure. Ajamu X's art is often categorised as "Black queer work", because of his identity and his subjects'. Even though Blackness and queerness are present, maybe even central, categorising his work within these identities is a very incomplete reading. Framing art sociologically is always limited; really, Ajamu is seeing how pleasure runs through, within and across our social identities. When he and I spoke, he talked about the "realm of imagination" and the "internal world".

Yes! I thought. *This is what's special about his work, and why it descends from Pierre's.*

The same can be said for all the work, from art to porn, that features a fetish. When a person with a fetish for feet takes hold of some kind of representation of their interest, they are accessing something held deeply inside them – their 'internal world'. The more I read from history, the further I reached into my own desire, and my understanding of it. This didn't kill it for me. Instead, it helped me to see it more as part of me, my nature, my interest and my glory. I could see more clearly the ways how forces from the world outside of my own body – from the Bible to Krafft-Ebing – might have shaped this internal part of me. Looking into the history helped me to find my freak, the one deep inside, and let him dance.

"I personally love smelly feet," Reed told me one day, surprising herself. "I've always loved smelly feet in the people that I've played with, especially women's feet." Reed knows she is unusual, as a woman into feet. When she found another one, she was blown away by her – they simply *had* to go on a couple of dates. "It's intoxicating, isn't it?" she said, about the connection we feel with someone with the same freak. These two women were able to access their internal worlds, exploring as they allowed the rest of the world to fall into silence.

Mark is similar. I was intrigued by him, of course; he's just a regular guy who doesn't make any kind of work to do with his fetish, instead it's just a part of his life. If Richard von Krafft-Ebing or Sigmund Freud had met him, they would have been keen to analyse him and categorise him. Mark is a true fetishist – his primary sexual interest is men's socks. You could even say that is his sexuality. Unknown to his loved ones, colleagues and neighbours, he has structured his life around his desire for used socks and shoes. "My flat's quite empty," he said, and I looked around. He was right. The man didn't even have any pictures on the walls. He was always just thinking about socks and shoes. "I don't buy anything else."

One day when I visited him, Mark was chuffed with a recent purchase. A 55-year-old truck driver had sold him a pair of boots at a bargain price of £50. "He did me a super special mega deal," Mark grinned. Gently, we talked about finances, and he told me about spending hundreds every month on socks and shoes. "I would prioritise the money on fetish over lamp shades or a replacement TV or a new coffee machine," he told me, before adding: "It's what I enjoy."

And I thought, *Why the fuck not?*

We all spend our money in ways that reveal our interests and our values. But, of course, I was intrigued by Mark's dedication. I was intrigued by how Reed was "blown away" with excitement at the sexual prospects with another woman who was into feet. The fact is that one in seven of us experience a fetish for feet – and the strength and prevalence of this human experience has always posed questions. That's what got the beard-strokers into the game. One way or another, we've continued to ask their questions. A century after the beard-strokers were working, a group of researchers based in Sweden and Italy, and led by Claudia Scorolli, surveyed 381 online discussion groups, collecting sexual preferences from at least 5,000 people. They wanted to know the relative frequency of different fetishes, and they found that feet and objects associated with feet, such as shoes and socks, were the most common target for our fetishistic desires.[50]

Other researchers have looked for the 'reason' behind our fetish for feet. If you search on Google for the causes of a foot fetish, it won't take long before you come across an idea from a neuroscientist called V. S. Ramachandran. Some of his most significant work has focused on phantom limbs, or the sensations that an amputated or missing limb is still there. By studying how a person's brain seems to produce a feeling in a body part that they've lost, Ramachandran has also made many insights into how we work. One insight is a map of the brain, showing that the part of the brain that processes sensory information from the genitals is next to the part that does the same job for the feet.

You can probably see where this is leading. Reporting in a scientific journal in 1998, Ramachandran said he'd looked at two patients who had each undergone the amputation of a foot. Both of them still felt sensation in their missing feet – their phantom limbs. These feelings arose when they had sex. And one of the two patients felt erotic sensations in his foot that made his orgasm bigger than it used to be. This interested Ramachandran, who had already noticed that the brain processes signals from the genitals and feet in adjacent areas. He speculated: "One wonders whether foot-fetishes in normal individuals may also result from such accidental 'cross wiring'."[51]

Later, in 2013, a group of scientists led by neuropsychologist Oliver Turnbull did a survey of our bodies' erogenous zones. Turnbull and his colleagues knew about Ramachandran's work, and what they found disputed it. Turnbull's study of 800 people, published in the journal *Cortex* in 2013, showed that statistically humans do not find feet erogenous to the touch, and that stimulating the brain where Ramachandran thought it would be pleasurable actually wasn't. They added that fetishes are actually a visual form of desire, not related to our sense of *touch*.[52]

This stopped me in my tracks. That wasn't because I was loyal to Ramachandran's ideas. No. I paused because I wanted to ask Turnbull roughly a thousand and one questions. I wasn't about to try to refute his statistical significance with my anecdotal evidence. But I did want to know how his finding stood up against the millennium's worth of drawings, stories and videos of people experiencing erogenous touch to their feet that I'd just sashayed through. And what about the *smells*?

Neither Turnbull nor Ramachandran denied the existence of our fetish for feet (and, unlike some, they didn't call it perverse). But they had *explained* it in a way that, ultimately, I found dissatisfying. Even though I was full of curiosity, after all the research into the actual experiences of people with a fetish for feet, I found the scientists' questions to be, well, wrong-footed.

I respect science, and the insights, technologies and medicines it brings us. But as I looked through a history of our fetish for feet, I found the scientific research and psycho-sexological ideas to be lacking. None of them came close to the insights offered by the writers, artists and performers who had given themselves to pleasure. If I was looking for an antidote to my shame, it came from the perverts, not the lab coats and beard-strokers. This is why it's good to explore the history, but misguided to be looking for the cause of our fetish for feet.

"It's not an important scientific question," Dug told me one day. "Who cares if you like blondes or redheads? You don't know why your body prefers that. It just does."

I couldn't refute that. Of course our desires are shaped by our experiences and society – ableism, racism, sexism can all play a role in who we fancy. It's worth interrogating

86

that… but feet? As I burrowed into my research, trying to understand myself and my body, I found the stories and the images much more compelling than the science. Dug wouldn't be surprised by this. He has spent decades helping thousands of people to discover and to experience the pleasure in their bodies, and he has no time for brain science or psychology. "If you want to do that," he said, "you go right ahead and spend your time doing that. To me, it's a waste of time. And we have such a short time on this planet. I'm just going to enjoy it."

The outside world stops so many of us from finding the freak inside. I am talking about other people, people trying to be *normal*, people who *create shame*. Shame is the way we are made to feel bad. Often we do this to ourselves.

I've discovered that I'm part of the same tradition as medieval toe-loving troubadours, Victorian weirdos, and curious creatures from the darkroom. What a family! Now I've found these ancestors, I will not feel bad about myself and my fetish. Humans have long had this sexual interest. The stories we tell about feet and sex have held us back from enjoying this desire. But the pleasure is inside us, waiting to bloom, and it is our beauty.

I'm on the floor and you are standing. I'm breathing hard and heavy.

Your foot hovers once more over my face, a hot surprise.

You push your sock against my cheek, my mouth, my nose. I am wedged between the floor and your foot.

I inhale, deep: the smell of your day, the smell of your foot, the smell of you. I can't get enough. I hear myself moan. My limbs fail, and I'm yours.

In finding something inside myself, for once in my life, I let go.

I am all yours.

References

Introduction

1   Tina Horn, *Why Are People Into That?* Hachette, 2024.
2   Ricky Martin's Big Secret, on Harry Connick, Jr.'s YouTube channel youtube.com/watch?v=83JYsyB7oq4. Accessed 10 September 2024.
3   "Darren Criss Got a Pedicure at Ricky Martin's House" Jimmy Kimmel Live, *YouTube*, 11 January 2018. youtube.com/watch?v=fF4I7-f3FzQ. Accessed 10 September 2024.
4   "Kourtney Kardashian indulges Travis Barker's foot fetish in cut-out red lingerie", Jess Phillips, *Daily Star*, 16 February 2024. dailystar.co.uk/showbiz/us-showbiz/kourtney-kardashian-indulges-travis-barkers-32132732. Accessed 10 September 2024.
5   "Lily Allen reveals the bizarre requests she's had since starting OnlyFans to make money off her feet and she says it's 'empowering' after being sexualised at a young age", Madison Burgess, *Daily Mail*, 9 July 2024. dailymail.co.uk/tvshowbiz/article-13615619/Lily-Allen-reveals-bizarre-requests-OnlyFans-feet.html. Accessed 10 September 2024.
6   "Love Island 2021: Jake Cornish secretly records toe sucking after revealing foot fetish and obviously viewers are shaken", Billie Schwab Dunn, *Metro*, 29 June 2021. metro.co.uk/2021/06/29/love-island-viewers-slam-jake-cornish-secretly-recording-toe-sucking-14843170/. Accessed 10 September 2024.
7   Richard von Krafft-Ebing, *Psychopathia Sexualis*. 1886.
8   Havelock Ellis, *Studies in the Psychology of Sex (vol 5)*. 1906.
9   Alfred Kinsey, *Sexual Behaviour in the Human Female*. Indiana University Press, 1953.
10   Ibid.

11   William A. Rossi, *The Sex Life of the Foot and Shoe*. Routledge and Keagan Paul, 1976.

12   Justin Lehmiller, *Tell Me What You Want*. Robinson, 2018. And "How Common Are Foot Fetishes, and Why Do People Have Them?" Justin Lehmiller and Zachary Zane, *Men's Health*, 7 October 2020. menshealth.com/sex-women/a19523651/foot-fetish/. Accessed 10 September 2024.

Chapter 1

13   Giannini AJ, Colapietro G, Slaby AE, Melemis SM, Bowman RK. Sexualization of the female foot as a response to sexually transmitted epidemics: a preliminary study. Psychol Rep. 1998 Oct;83(2):491-8. doi: 10.2466/pr0.1998.83.2.491. PMID: 9819924.

14   Howard S Levy, *Chinese Footbinding: The History of a Curious Erotic Custom*. Neville Spearman, 1967.

15   Ibid.

16   "1995.107: The Great Orgy of Maharao Shatru Sal II" Harvard Art Museums. hvrd.art/o/310594. Accessed 10 September 2024.

17   Andrew Graham-Dixon, "Caravaggio". *Encyclopedia Britannica*, 20 August 2024. britannica.com/biography/Caravaggio. Accessed 10 September 2024.

18   "The Project Gutenberg eBook of The Memoires of Casanova, by Jacques Casanova de Seingalt". gutenberg.org/files/2981/2981-h/2981-h.htm. Accessed 10 September 2024.

19   "Demons Licking Your Toes: An Early 20th Century Manuscript from Isfahan", Ali Karjoo-Ravary, *AJ Media Collective*, 31 October 2017. ajammc.com/2017/10/31/demons-licking-toes/. Accessed 10 September 2024.

20   "Footwear - United States", *Statista*. statista.com/outlook/cmo/footwear/united-states. Accessed 10 September 2024.

21   Salvatore Ferragamo, *Shoemaker of Dreams*. Rizzoli Electa, 1957.

22   Emily Sisley and Bertha Harris, *The Joy of Lesbian Sex*. Crown Publishers, 1977.

Chapter 2

23 Richard von Krafft-Ebing, *Psychopathia Sexualis*. 1886.
24 Comment by the editors of the British Medical Journal quoted in the second edition of the first authorised English translation of *Psychopathia Sexualis*, 1893.
25 "The Pearl (1879–1881), Printed for the Society of Vice", *Wikisource*. en.wikisource.org/wiki/The_Pearl. Accessed 10 September 2024.
26 G. Stanley Hall. "Some Aspects of the Early Sense of Self." *The American Journal of Psychology*, vol. 9, no. 3, 1898, pp. 351–95. JSTOR, https://doi.org/10.2307/1411300. Accessed 10 September 2024.
27 Havelock Ellis, *Studies in the Psychology of Sex (vol 1)*. 1897.
28 "That Foot Fetish Scene Was *House of the Dragon* At Its Most Shameless", Lauren Puckett-Pope, *Elle*, 17 October 2022. elle.com/culture/movies-tv/a41651192/house-of-the-dragon-foot-scene-larys-alicent/. Accessed 10 September 2024.
29 "*House of the Dragon* director reveals who was responsible for foot fetish scene" Dan Selcke, *Winter Is Coming*, 17 October 2022. winteriscoming.net/2022/10/17/house-of-the-dragon-director-reveals-who-responsible-foot-fetish-larys-strong-alicent-scene/. Accessed 10 September 2024.
30 "Foot fetish pervert climbed under seats at Leeds cinema and sexually assaulted girls as they watched *Dumbo*", Tony Gardner, *Yorkshire Evening Post*, 1 July 2019. yorkshireeveningpost.co.uk/news/crime/foot-fetish-pervert-climbed-under-seats-at-leeds-cinema-and-sexually-assaulted-girls-as-they-watched-dumbo-391383. Accessed 10 September 2024.
31 "Margot Robbie, John Cena & James Gunn on The Suicide Squad, Margot & John's History & Crazy Stunts", Jimmy Kimmel Live, *YouTube*, 22 July 2021. youtube.com/watch?v=l-umG06tKGU&t=483s. Accessed 10 September 2024.
32 "I don't hear from eligible bachelors on social media, just foot fetishists, says Hollyoaks star Jennifer Metcalfe", Susan Hill, *The Sun*, 8 October 2022. thesun.co.uk/tv/20046795/hollyoaks-star-jennifer-metcalfe-foot-fetishists/. Accessed 10 September 2024.

Chapter 3

33 Sigmund Freud, *Three Essays on the Theory of Sexuality*. Franz Deuticke, 1905.

34 Sigmund Freud (1927) Fetishism. *The Standard Edition of the Complete Psychological Works of Sigmund Freud* 21:147-158. pep-web.org/browse/document/se.021.0147a?page=P0147. Accessed 10 September 2024.

35 Wilhelm Stekel, *Sexual Abberations: The Phenomena of Fetishism in Relation to Sex*. John Lane The Bodley Head, 1930.

36 Emily Apter, *Feminising the Fetish: Psychoanalysis and Narrative Obsession in Turn-Of-The-Century France*. Cornell University Press, 1991.

37 Leezah Hertzmann and Juliet Newbigin (eds), *Sexuality and Gender Now Moving Beyond Heteronormativity*. Routledge, 2020.

38 Jane C. Czyzselska (ed), *Queering Psychotherapy*. Karnac Books, 2022.

Chapter 4

39 Tina Horn, *Why Are People Into That?* Hachette, 2024.

40 "Toe Poke: Why Is Foot Fetishism Stepping into the Spotlight?" Madeleine Pollard, *Elephant Art*, 7 October 2022. elephant.art/toe-poke-why-is-foot-fetishism-stepping-into-the-spotlight-07102022/. Accessed 10 September 2024.

41 Interview with Etienne held at the Leather Archive and Museum, Chicago. leatherarchives.org/the-man-behind-the-canvas. Accessed 10 September 2024.

42 "Pierre Molinier, the forgotten Surrealist", Iain Gale, *The Independent*, 4 November 1993. independent.co.uk/arts-entertainment/pierre-molinier-the-forgotten-surrealist-1502015.html. Accessed 10 September 2024.

43 William A. Rossi, *The Sex Life of the Foot and Shoe*. Routledge and Keagan Paul, 1976.

44 "Toe Poke: Why Is Foot Fetishism Stepping into the Spotlight?" Madeleine Pollard, *Elephant Art*, 7 October 2022. elephant.art/toe-poke-why-is-foot-fetishism-stepping-into-the-spotlight-07102022/. Accessed 10 September 2024.

45   PornHub insights, 2023. pornhub.com/insights/
2023-year-in-review#categories. Accessed 10 September
2024.

46   Grindr Unwrapped, 2023. grindr.com/unwrapped.
Accessed 10 September 2024.

47   "OnlyFans now has more than 3 million content creators
and is a 'global business', says the CEO", Jyoti Mann,
Business Insider, 13 May 2023. businessinsider.com/onlyfans-
has-more-than-3-million-creators-global-business-2023-5.
Accessed 10 September 2024.

48   "Selling his sole! Arizona man says he earns $4,000 a month
peddling 'sexy' FOOT pictures online after racking up thousands of followers on OnlyFans", *Mail Online*, 14 January
2021. dailymail.co.uk/femail/article-9147483/Man-makes-
4-000-month-selling-sexy-photos-FEET.html. Accessed 10
September 2024.

Conclusion

49   Tina Horn, *Why Are People Into That?*. Hachette, 2024.

50   Scorolli, C., Ghirlanda, S., Enquist, M. et al. Relative
prevalence of different fetishes. *Int J Impot Res* 19,
432–437 (2007). doi.org/10.1038/sj.ijir.3901547.
Accessed 10 September 2024.

51   Ramachandran VS, Hirstein W. The perception of phantom limbs. The D. O. Hebb lecture. Brain. 1998 Sep;121
(Pt 9):1603-30. doi: 10.1093/brain/121.9.1603. PMID:
9762952.

52   Oliver Turnbull et al, Reports of intimate touch: Erogenous
zones and somatosensory cortical organization. *Cortex*, 2013.

Acknowledgements

Books have a big adventure as they grow from an idea in the writer's mind into the pile of words you can hold in your hand. There are two groups of people who I especially want to thank for supporting *Solemates* on its journey. The first is Will Nutland, Dale Taylor-Gentles, Grant Gulczynski and everyone else at The Love Tank, Rich Mix, and Fringe! Queer Film & Arts Fest. They gave me space to assemble some research and ideas into an event in September 2023. I worked with the energetic performers Lori lo Bianco, Reece Connolly and Co Kendrah to give the audience a fun time, all about feet!, and it boosted me with the confidence to pursue this project and keep building the idea.

The second group is Heather and Laura from 404 Ink. They instantly understood my idea, affirmed it, and gave me a runway to write. They orchestrated the Kickstarter and publicity campaign around the series of Inklings that this book is a part of. And, crucially, they edited the book into the right form and shape, making sure to place its arguments in their best light.

Thank you to the other residents and excellent staff at Arteles Creative Centre in Haukijärvi, Finland. I was on a residency there in 2022 when I did the early work on this project, discovering what I wanted to say about our fetish for feet. Another space to think and write was provided by Mo Hafeez, so thank you, Mo.

I drew on the expertise and collections at Bishopsgate Institute in London and the Leather Archive & Museum in Chicago. Thanks to the archivists there for this, and all the important work you do in collecting things that pertain to our sexual imaginations (not an easy job!). To the booksellers who would look at a book like this and give it a punt: thank you, you dreamboats.

I'm indebted to Ajamu X, Dug Gaines, Mark, and Reed Amber. You opened up, you trusted me with your stories, and we had some very informative conversations. We are family.

Finally, I'm grateful to all the people who have found the freak inside themselves, and in me. To the bedroom playmates, the basement piggies, the darkroom honeys, and the pleasure pervs who post the wildest things online: thank you, keep exploring, and go well x

About the Author

Credit: India Latham

Adam Zmith is a writer and podcast producer whose work explores the beats of our bodies, in the past, present and future. He is the author of *Deep Sniff: A History of Poppers and Queer Futures* (Repeater Books, 2021), which won the Polari First Book Prize, 2022. As a writer he has also made work for theatre and film. In podcasts, he co-produced *The Log Books*, wrote and produced the BBC series *The Film We Can't See*, hosts *Free Sex*, and is co-director of the production company Aunt Nell.

    adamzmith.com
    X: @adamzmith
    Instagram: @adam.zmith

About the Inklings series

This book is part of 404 Ink's Inkling series which presents big ideas in pocket-sized books.

They are all available at 404ink.com/shop.

If you enjoyed this book, you may also enjoy these titles in the series:

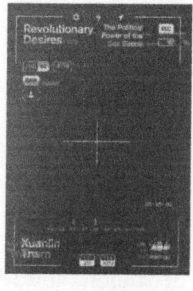

Revolutionary Desires – Xuanlin Tham

Cinema is becoming less and less sexy; yet more and more people are rallying against sex on screen. Why is the sex scene, demonised as it is, therefore more politically important and subversive than ever? *Revolutionary Desires* seeks to answer that question.

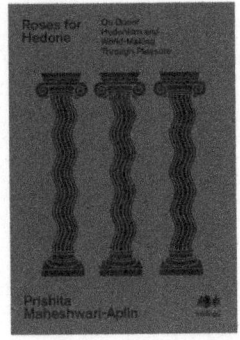

Roses for Hedone – Prishita Maheshwari-Aplin

As we face ongoing and new challenges to creating a fairer world, let us borrow from the Ancient Greeks' understanding of love's multiplicity to explore queer hedonism not as a momentary phenomenon, but rather a transformational route through which we can learn from our past, connect in the present, and look towards the future with hope – together.

Look, Don't Touch – layla-roxanne hill & Francesca Sobande

Look, Don't Touch journeys through the music of feeling, "self-help" social media, the power of public signage, and more to call for a move away from the language of "okayness", and a move towards collectively uplifting forms of anger, agitation, love, solidarity, release, and ultimately, *feeling*.